Dear One,

Bless You!

Ron Palumbo

Using the

Law of Attraction

WISELY

*The book with both the information AND The TOOLS
to GREATLY IMPROVE Your Life*

Ron Palumbo

BALBOA.
PRESS

A DIVISION OF HAY HOUSE

Balboa Press books may be ordered through booksellers or by contacting:

Balboa Press
A Division of Hay House
1663 Liberty Drive
Bloomington, IN 47403
www.balboapress.com
1 (877) 407-4847

Because of the dynamic nature of the Internet, any web addresses or links contained in this book may have changed since publication and may no longer be valid. The views expressed in this work are solely those of the author and do not necessarily reflect the views of the publisher, and the publisher hereby disclaims any responsibility for them.

The author of this book does not dispense medical advice or prescribe the use of any technique as a form of treatment for physical, emotional, or medical problems without the advice of a physician, either directly or indirectly. The intent of the author is only to offer information of a general nature to help you in your quest for emotional and spiritual well-being. In the event you use any of the information in this book for yourself, which is your constitutional right, the author and the publisher assume no responsibility for your actions.

Any people depicted in stock imagery provided by Thinkstock are models, and such images are being used for illustrative purposes only. Certain stock imagery © Thinkstock.

Printed in the United States of America.

Library of Congress Control Number: 2014902975

ISBN: 978-1-4525-9265-7 (sc)
ISBN: 978-1-4525-9267-1 (hc)
ISBN: 978-1-4525-9266-4 (e)

Library of Congress Control Number: 2014902975

Balboa Press rev. date: 5/16/2014

Contents

Chapter 1

Discovering the Law of Attraction… the Basis of All Empowerment Workshops

Learn as if you'll live forever.
Mahatma Gandhi

Throughout history, humankind has sought to discover, understand, and live in harmony with "the powers that be."

In ancient times, due to an ignorance of nature and natural phenomena, various communities attributed powers to various gods and goddesses. Throughout tens of thousands of years of evolution and of a growing in awareness, many now understand there is a governing force… a Higher Power… a Divine Presence… an Absolute Truth.

We humans have heard, read, or studied various paths and belief systems that "touch on" Absolute Truth. While our attempts have been sincere, we have danced around Absolute Truth since our beginning, never quite hitting the mark. This lack of understanding about the

"BIG PICTURE of Life" is partly due to our human ego, but also because of other limitations as well.

Our human ego, coupled with our human misunderstanding of Absolute Truth has created confusion and exclusiveness. It is a big part of our total misunderstanding of "The BIG PICTURE" of life.

So instead of living life ABUNDANTLY (what this author calls the Celebration of Life), humankind throughout history has experienced struggle and strife in many life areas.

A New Beginning

Always eager to learn and grow, I "stumbled upon" a couple of life-changing tools and techniques more than 25 years ago. One of the tools had such a profound impact on my life that, when a friend was going through a dry spell of not getting any work, I shared this empowering process with him. As the sole financial support for his family of four, his lack of work was creating a serious financial challenge. The result: within ten (10) days of sharing this process with him, two of his work bids were accepted.

His workmanship was of such high quality, that prior to the completion of these two jobs, he had two additional clients who also wanted him to do remodeling projects on their homes.

A short time later, an acquaintance was going through several challenges in her life. She was barely making ends meet financially. Her car was often needing repairs, she wasn't really happy with her job, and she had to drive about an hour each morning to get to work.

After she told me about her challenges, I shared the same process with her.

Within one week, her entire attitude on life had improved and her work situation became extremely positive. She accepted a position to write grant proposals for a nonprofit. They would provide an office that was only thirty miles away from her home, or she could work out of her home. Another huge benefit for her was that her starting salary that was 150 percent of her previous salary.

Prior to these two events, I knew how empowering and life-changing these tools were because I had a profound experience upon my using them. But after the immediate life improvement experiences of these two friends, I knew I had to share this information with everyone.

So I called several churches, asking if they had a Divorce Recovery Group. If they did, I offered to give a FREE Evening Program to that group. Several churches accepted this offer. In their group meeting I shared the most important tools for people who've been hurt, a process that releases old hurts once and for all. Then I shared the process that releases ALL negative energy between you and any other person… alive or dead.

The wonderful feedback that came back to me inspired me to offer classes at community colleges, service groups, churches, professional associations, and many locations outside of my home town. Over the years, our workshop continued to evolve and grow.

For more than a dozen years, many attendees have stated that our workshop is "the most powerful workshop" they'd ever attended.

Attendees from "Using the Law of Attraction WISELY" workshop who continued to **"Do The Work"** that we begin in our workshop… these folks have experienced huge breakthroughs in all life areas.

"The Work" can be done in about 15 to 20 minutes each day.

"Do the Work and your life improves. There are NO EXCEPTIONS!"

From the very beginning of facilitating our workshop over twenty-five years ago, we began receiving unsolicited testimonials and thank you letters (many of which shared their success stories). Within a short time, so many letters had arrived that we filled an entire file storage box with them.

Many shared they had an immediate increase in income. Many had physical, relationship, financial, and other types of healings.

A woman who attended our workshop in Dallas, TX in early 1989 sent me a thank you letter a few months afterwards. Her letter shared she is a health instructor for a large company, and instructors are graded on how many people signed up for the next series of classes. Her letter stated, "Prior to attending your workshop, my sales percentage had consistently been "mediocre" (in the mid-70's). But after attending your workshop and **applying the techniques**, I skyrocketed to 98%… and have been in the 90's ever since. And I have a whole new outlook on life."

Three years later, I was a featured speaker at a National Healing Symposium in Kansas City, and this woman attended this event. She reintroduced herself to me and told me that after attending our workshop, she became the top sales person for her national company in 1989 and was awarded a new car.

For years people have told me our workshop was the "most powerful" or "the best" they'd ever attended. One chiropractor in Florida stated that it was, "the most powerful thing I've ever experienced in my life!" He said his life "literally went from the 'pits of hell' to something out of Fantasy Island."

"Do the work... your life improves! There are NO EXCEPTIONS!"

This has been our guarantee for over twenty-five years!

And for over twenty-five years, the people who continued to do the work that we begin in our workshop have experienced huge improvements in several areas of life!

Here's an empowering suggestion. Don't just read this book, *live* with it.

While reading this book will help you better understand why life happens the way it does, as well as give you the tools to transform your consciousness, there is much more to life than merely understanding it intellectually.

Learning things intellectually is just that. It is *only* learning!

Making a change in our consciousness (changing our thoughts, words, and actions) requires more from us than just learning about something.

Transformation requires growing; it requires change!

Without growth, we are stagnant. Life cannot exist without growth. Always go for the growth.

We are all here to learn and grow, and we're all capable of growing. After all, whether we know it or not, we are Empowered beings!

We have the ability to greatly improve our life by using the tools and techniques in this book.

So I challenge you to do the work and improve your life.

Be the awesome, empowered being you were created to be.

The tools to help you be this empowered person are in this book.

Please use the tools that are here for you.

Do the work and your life improves!

There are no exceptions!

Chapter 2

Using the Law of Attraction WISELY Empowers Us

Self-awareness is the first step toward Self-Mastery.

Ron Palumbo

Our Using the Law of Attraction WISELY workshop includes both of the ingredients necessary to effectively transform one's consciousness, and thus, transform and greatly improve one's life. Our workshop gives attendees the information and tools to transform consciousness.

The information gives attendees a much better understanding of the big picture of life, how life works, and why it unfolds the way it does.

The tools in our Empowerment Workbook greatly accelerate an individual's ability to remove all of the Bad Programming ("the garbage") from his/her subconscious mind.

Here's an illustration explaining how and why our workshop empowers people.

Think of a light bulb. Light bulbs radiate light outward in all directions, 360 degrees by 360 degrees. This light is called **Scattered** or **Diffused** light, because the light energy goes out everywhere in all directions. This is a perfect example of scattered energy.

Illustration #1- Scattered Energy: A Light Bulb sends out light energy in all directions: 360 degrees x 360 degrees

If we take this same light energy and focus it into a single beam, it is now directed in a Single Phase. This is now a focused energy and is so powerful it can cut through (or burn through) most substances.

We call this Single Phase beam of light a laser. It is a very powerful, focused energy!

Illustration #2- Focused Energy: A laser directs light energy in a **single phase (one single line)**. It's **focused energy** can cut through or burn through many materials

Most humans are much like a light bulb with our personal energy. Our energy goes all over the place, in several directions at the same time, to the point where we are often in direct opposition to ourselves and to our intended goals and directions. This is because we send out opposing energies simultaneously.

We'll cover this in great detail later in this book.

Chapter 3

Know the Truth... and the Truth sets us free

Let us make humankind in our image and likeness; and let them have *dominion* over (everything).

Genesis 1:26

We live in a world of energy and a universe of energy. Everything in the physical universe, both the visible and the invisible, is made up of energy.

From the movement of galaxies to the movement of subatomic particles, and everything in between, all energy follows one great dynamic process. This dynamic process is called the law of attraction! Because this dynamic is so encompassing, some metaphysicians merely call it "The Law."

Just as Mathematical Principle governs the calculations of numbers, so too, the law of attraction is the dynamic that governs the flow of all energy.

Understanding how life works is the first step in improving your life experience. Having the tools to do the work (to remove "the garbage" from our subconscious mind) is the knowing step. Then being disciplined enough to actually do the work is the action step. (There is a huge difference between *knowing* what to do and actually *doing* what is ours to do).

"Doing the Work" is the Action Step that allows us to use our energy WISELY.

Please recall our illustration of the light bulb verses the laser at the end of Chapter Two. The light bulbs sends out light energy out in all directions (Scattered or Diffused Energy). Whereas the laser puts the light energy into a single phase so that it is a focused energy, powerful enough to burn through substances.

Our Empowerment Workshops help people go from scattered energy to a focused energy. As all of our energies (all of our thoughts, words, and actions) come into harmony, and are in alignment in the same direction, then we can move (or remove) mountains in our life.

This is the reason why workshop attendees who "Do the Work" have had, what several of them have called, "miracles" in their lives.

Please note: I do not call these events miracles. Rather, I totally agree with Eric Butterworth, one of the greatest metaphysicians of the 20th Century, who often stated: "There are NO miracles! What we humans call a miracle is merely the application of a higher law than what we're aware of in any given situation."

Most people on Classroom Earth send out scattered energy continuously, thus people mostly misdirect their energy.

After attending our workshop, some of the attendees continue to "Do the Work" that we begin in our workshop. As folks continue the process of eliminating the blockages (the Bad Programming) in their subconscious, they better focus their energy toward whatever their goals are, and thus experience tremendous breakthroughs in various life areas.

This will also be true for the *readers* of this book who go beyond just learning about energy. As readers go into the action step, they become *doers* of the work.

As you do the work (the exercises) in this book, you, too, will become more centered, more clear, and more focused in your energy output. As your energy becomes more focused, you become more empowered. It's really that simple.

Empowered people work more effectively and more efficiently, thus work performance improves. As work performance improves, in general, income increases.

Most of the feedback mail I've received from workshop attendees is their gratitude and joy over their increased income.

Life was designed for us to live abundantly. We were created to live life abundantly. The only thing holding us back is the vast amount of bad programming ("garbage") in our subconscious mind. Once it is removed, we are empowered and we enjoy life at a higher level of all good.

Empowered people are more considerate of others, thus their relationships are often enhanced. This includes not only their primary relationship with their spouse/life partner, but also several attendees reported healings of relationships with loved ones, some of which were adversarial prior to attending our workshop.

Empowered people are more open to the flow of life energy throughout their bodies because they have less blockages. Energy blockages diminish the flow of life energy to our body's cells, organs, and tissues. As we remove the blockages, life energy flows freely throughout our body temples. Upon "Doing the Work" several former workshop attendees reported physical healings. Another direct result of taking the action step (doing the work) is living at a higher level of health and wholeness.

The good news is everyone can become empowered! Everyone was created to be empowered! So within every person is everything needed to be the empowered human being we were created to be.

The only question to ask is: Am I willing to "Do the Work" it takes for me to live life more abundantly?

If so, congratulations to you!

You have the right attitude to improve your life.

You're willing to take 15 minutes each day to **"Do the Work"** that will transform your consciousness... and thus, improve your life.

In addition to having the right attitude to improve your life, you now have the other vital piece needed to transform your consciousness. You are holding in your hand the book that contains both the information... **and the tools** needed to **"Do the Work!"**

Chapter 4

We Live In a World Of Energy

To see a world in a grain of sand
And a heaven in a wild flower
Hold infinity in the palm of your hand
And eternity in an hour

William Blake

We live in a world of energy. Everything in the physical universe is made up of energy. Even things that "appear" to be solid are made up of energy, and this energy is always in motion at the subatomic level.

The two types of physical energy we'll address in this book are: visible energy (i.e. table, chair, car), and invisible energy (i.e. light, sound, gasses, vapors).

Visible Energy appears to be solid (i.e. a table, chair, building, etc.).

Objects that seem to be solid maintain their solid pattern unless acted upon by another energy, either visible or invisible energy.

However there are more levels of energy in our world than just the two types of physical energy previously mentioned.

We humans exist on four (4) levels of being: mental, emotional, physical, and spiritual.

And we humans emit energy on all four levels of being.

People are made up of energy. In fact, humans are all about energy. We are energy receivers and energy transmitters. Scientists have stated that humans transmit and receive over 60,000 energy transmissions within our body every day.

In the first chapter of Genesis, God gave us dominion over everything!

The "everything" we have dominion over is our own personal energy!

This includes our thoughts, our words, our actions, and our feelings.

Yes! In spite of what many people say and think, we have complete dominion over our feelings.

Shaping our personal energy, which is immediately directed out into the universe, is how we humans create our life's experiences.

Truth-based, positive affirmations are a powerful way to help us wake up to Truth, the Truth that sets us free. So please utilize the power of affirmations to help transform your consciousness, and hence, improve your life.

So I suggest you say the following affirmation OUT LOUD!

Affirm: I create my life by shaping and directing energy!

Immediately after stating an affirmation, take a moment to rest in the energy of what you've just affirmed. "Breathe in" what you've just stated, pausing in the silence for a moment or two. Allow the energy of your words to resonate throughout your entire body.

For those of us who are aware of the power of affirmations (the power of the spoken word), and who are OPEN to use affirmations to more quickly facilitate our transformation of consciousness, **please affirm out loud:**

**I have complete dominion over
my personal energy!**
(pause for 2 or 3 breaths, allowing the
energy to resonate within you)

Because affirmations are an effective, powerful tool to accelerate the transformation of consciousness, I will suggest them throughout this book. Whenever you see the phrase, **"Please affirm out loud"** written in bold type, an affirmation will immediately follow.

I invite you to say the affirmation out loud, and to take a few seconds (a few relaxed breathes) of silence afterwards, thus allowing the energy of your affirmation to resonate throughout your body.

An affirmation more effectively sinks into our consciousness when we pause (relax in the silence) immediately after stating the affirmation out loud. This gives our body time to allow the energy of our thoughts and words to resonate within our body's energy field. Given these few seconds of silence after an affirmation, our body's energy field assimilates and resonates with the energy of our thoughts and words. Our body harmonizes with the energy of our affirmation as it incorporates the wisdom / high Truth of the affirmation into our consciousness.

The energy of our affirmation immediately goes out to the universe. Because we live in a friendly universe, whatever energy we send out, the universe can only say "YES" to this energy, and then send this same energy back to us (the sender).

Our personal energy (the energy we shape and send out to the Universe) is how we create all of our life's experiences.

This book gives the information about our personal energy (how we shape, direct, and mostly MISDIRECT energy). It also gives the tools and techniques that will clean out the garbage from our subconscious mind, and thus help us to become more empowered.

As we "Do the Work" we will find ourselves using our energy more wisely than ever before!

Using our energy wisely is the real secret to experiencing higher levels of health, happiness, fulfillment, and living life abundantly (which includes living in bliss).

Health and wholeness is the natural result of energy flowing freely throughout our body temple, unblocked and unrestricted. So health and wholeness are also a result of using our energy wisely!

Effectively s-l-o-w-i-n-g the aging process happens as we allow the body's energy to flow freely to all systems, organs, and cells. This allows our life energy to do what it was designed to do, to renew and heal our cells *continuously*!

Everybody shapes and directs energy continuously. Unfortunately, most people also misdirect energy continuously.

Think of a time when you encountered someone who drains your energy. This can happen when we experience people who lower our energy. Not only can it happen when we are in the presence of this person, but also it can even happen when talking with him/her on the phone.

We have also experienced being in the presence of an uplifting person, someone who is delightful to be with and whose energy literally uplifts and inspires us. Their positive energy affects us by raising our energy level.

As we become more aware of our dominion over our personal energy, and as we become more responsible of the energy we are sending out, we begin to use our energy more wisely.

All people are energy transmitters and energy receivers. To make this point more clear for our workshop attendees, one of the wonderful exercises everyone experiences near the beginning of our workshop is the sending and the receiving of energy.

I invite all attendees to be aware of their feelings in both the sending and receiving of energy as they participate in a brief exercise. Upon completing the exercise we discuss the feelings that were felt throughout the exercise. Attendees who shared their experience about our group exercise acknowledged and described the various positive feelings they felt as they sent and received energy with our group.

By the end of the exercise and the group discussion afterwards, all workshop attendees were fully aware that everyone transmits and receives energy every day, throughout each day.

Shaping and directing our personal energy is how we create our life's experiences.

Please affirm out loud:

> **I create my life's experiences by**
> **shaping and directing energy.**
> ... (pause)

> **I use my energy WISELY... and I**
> **am blessed in all areas of life.**
> ... (pause)

Remember, pausing in the silence for a few seconds immediately after stating an affirmation allows our body time to resonate in the energy field we just created by our affirmation. As our body assimilates and resonates with this energy, it harmonizes with this energy. In doing so, we give our body the opportunity to incorporate the wisdom / higher Truth of our words into our consciousness.

Chapter 5

The Flow of Life
The Dynamics of Energy

We live in a friendly universe.

Albert Einstein

The universe is designed to always support us. It supports us by totally supporting whatever energy we send out to it. No matter what energy we send out, the universe always says "YES!" to our energy. Thus, the universe always supports our energy perfectly!

Throughout various periods of my life I consciously interacted and/or played with personal energy.

As a child I became aware of some amazing things regarding energy. Being a musician at a very early age, music has always been a huge joy for me.

Although this event happened decades ago, I still clearly recall it and the tremendous effect it had on me for the rest of my life.

This event happened while I was in my teens (about 14 years of age) on a day when everything was going along nicely. I began singing one of the popular songs of the day. After singing this song, I became aware that I was feeling a bit sad.

I clearly recalled that I was not feeling sad before singing this song.

Aware of the change in my feelings, I wondered if the song that I sang (which had a sad theme) was the reason I now didn't feel as good as I had felt before singing the song with all it's sad verses.

But even more importantly, I wondered what might happen if, on a day I was not feeling too good, but sang a happy song (in spite of my feelings), would the happy song help me to feel better?

I could hardly wait to experiment (explore and resolve this possibility) in real life.

But there was a challenge. I began looking for a happy song in order to have it ready the next time I was being punished for something, or didn't do well on a test in school, or, in general, my energy level was low.

My first realization was that it took a while for me to even find a happy song! Most of our popular songs on the radio were usually sad songs. They were about losing our girlfriend/boyfriend to someone else, and missing him/her, or about not being with the person we love, or being in intense pain over the loss of our loved one, and things of a sad nature.

After some effort, I finally found a happy song.

And a few weeks later, it finally happened. Mom restricted me to my bedroom, thus couldn't go outside, nor have any friends visit our home. It meant I had to spend time in my bedroom.

This situation made me feel sad, *until* I remembered my *experiment*.

So, I sang my *happy song*.

WOW!!!

I could hardly believe it. **I felt GREAT!**

It worked!

We affect our emotional state of mind by our thoughts and our words!

This childhood discovery clearly showed me that we have the ability to raise, or lower our energy level based on our thoughts. In general, singing happy songs lifts our spirits (lifts our energy), whereas singing sad songs lowers our spirits (lowers our energy).

Many years later I further learned WHY singing songs impacts us so profoundly. It does so because singing engages our emotional nature, and our emotional nature *a*mplifies whatever energy we are transmitting. This happens because, in addition to engaging our mental nature, it also engages our emotional nature. Additionally, we increases the intensity of our physical nature when we speak or sing out loud.

No matter what energy we transmit into the universe, the universe always responds in one way. It always says "YES!" to our energy.

The two states of energy we deal with regarding the Law of Attraction are:

1. Universal Energy
2. Directed Energy

Universal Energy is unshaped, non-directed, neutral energy. It has neither a positive nor a negative charge.[1] It is totally unshaped energy, and thus is shaped by the consciousness around it.

Universal Energy (henceforth written as UE) is everywhere present throughout the universe! It is present at the sub-atomic level, throughout Classroom Earth, throughout space, and throughout the entire physical universe.

UE adapts to the energy field (the consciousness) around it. The consciousness around UE shapes and molds it into an exact replica of the consciousness that shaped it. Once shaped, it is now transformed into **Directed Energy.** (See "psychometry" in the Definition of Terms at the end of this book).

Directed Energy (henceforth written as DE) was formerly UE that has been acted upon by an outside force, thus, transformed it into shaped energy (DE). It now has a charge, usually either positive or negative, however it can also be a somewhat neutral charge when the DE is neither a positive nor a negative charge.

For example, choosing to go to the beach would be a neutral energy, if you have the time and the means to do so, and you are not shortchanging any other obligations in your life.

Directed Energy has been shaped, therefore it now has a "charge," and, thus, a mission.

Once having a mission, DE goes out to *the Universe* to fulfill its mission.

DE always fulfills its mission!

It doesn't matter if the energy is positive, or negative. The *Universe* always says "YES" to Directed Energy.

At an energy level all people are conduits for energy. Just as a garden hose or PCV pipe is a conduit for water, so too has our body temple been created to be a conduit for energy.

Every person is a channel that shapes, transmits, and receives energy.

Following is an illustration of how energy flows: how we shape it, how we transmit it, how the Universe says "YES!" to our energy, and then sends it back to us.

I call this dynamic process *The Flow of Life.*

(Illustrations 3, 4, and 5 show how the *Flow of Life* process unfolds).

Each person is a vessel for the *Flow of Life.* Each of us is like a piece of garden hose or PVC pipe.

Illustration #3- The "Flow of Life"... each person is a channel for energy. Unshaped Universal Energy is shaped by our thoughts... & sent out to the universe.

Whatever thoughts we are thinking and whatever words we are saying, these thoughts and words "impregnate" the Universal Energy (they transform it and give it a charge). This newly-shaped energy reflects our consciousness at the time, transforming the Universal Energy (UE or Unshaped Energy) into Directed Energy (which is now Shaped Energy, has a charge, and has a mission).

Illustration #4- The "Flow of Life" continued. The universe says "YES" to our energy... & sends it back to the sender.

The Universe always says "YES!" to our Shaped Energy and then sends this same energy back to us, which completes its mission.

This process is how we co-create (manifest) our life experiences.

We shape Unshaped Energy, transforming into Directed Energy, and send it out to the universe. This is our part of the co-creative process.

Then the Universe says "YES" to our Directed Energy and sends it back to us fulfilled. (See Illustration 5, below).

The Universe completes the co-creative process (sending back the same energy we sent out). This process is known by various names and descriptions.

Some of the names and descriptions for this process include: karma, the circle of life, "be it done unto you according to your faith," - "whatever you sow you shall reap," and other terms and descriptions as well.

The universe, sending our Directed Energy back to us fulfilled is how we *reap what we have sown.*

```
Illustration #5 - The Flow of Life - Mission Fulfilled
In this illustration, "love" thoughts shape and transform
the Unshaped Universal Energy into a Directed Energy of
love.
The Directed Energy of love goes out to the universe.
The Universe says "YES!" to Directed Energy... and then
sends the exact same energy back to the sender.  The
Directed Energy's mission has been fulfilled.
```

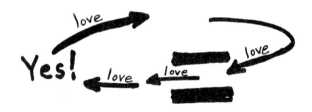

Illustrations #3, 4, and 5 show the "Flow of Life" process as it unfolds.

We shape energy by our thoughts. Our thoughts transform Universal Energy into Directed Energy. Directed Energy goes out into the Universe (Illustration #3).

The Universe says "YES" to our Directed Energy… then sends that same energy back to us (Illustrations #4 and 5).

Because we shape energy with our total consciousness... our conscious words are only *part* of this "Flow of Life" process.

The basis of the Law of Attraction is thoughts held in our mind give form and shape to the Unshaped Universal Energy that is everywhere present. UE is everywhere present throughout the physical universe.

Another aspect of Energy shaped by thoughts

Our thoughts, words and actions, depending on our level of HARMONY within our consciousness, can either enhance (speed up) OR slow the "Flow of Life" process. As we become more focused with our energy we shorten the length of time it takes for the Universe to send our Directed Energy back to us fulfilled.

We GREATLY Accelerate the "Flow of Life" process when our thoughts and feelings are FOCUSED. When focused, our thoughts and feelings are in Total HARMONY with ONE ANOTHER.[2]

The result of this harmony is that the "Flow of Life" process is quickened, so it takes less time for the shaped energy (DE) to return to us fulfilled.

This is why it is said that we co-create. The Divine (the Creative Universal Force / God) is the Source of all energy, including the unshaped Universal Energy. We humans utilize this Universal Energy as we transform it into Directed Energy and send it out to be fulfilled.

Thus most metaphysicians say that we "co-create with the Divine."

Directed Energy always has a mission!

Once Directed Energy is sent out into "the universe" it always fulfills the intention of the charge it now carries, regardless of whether it is a positive or a negative charge. Directed Energy always completes its mission! When Directed Energy returns to the "sender" its mission is accomplished!

This "Flow of Life" dynamic is how the Law of Attraction operates. It is how we shape, direct, and mostly misdirect energy. Whatever energy we send out to the universe, regardless of if it is positive or negative energy, this energy comes back to the sender, thus fulfilling its mission.

With the above statement in mind, why is it that we can say the right affirmations throughout the day... and yet, that which we are affirming doesn't manifest in our life?

For example, many people attend workshops on various topics. Let's use a prosperity workshop for an example. Most prosperity workshops focus on the use of affirmations.

While affirmations are a valid component of creating a consciousness of prosperity, many people have used affirmations alone did not experience any change in their level of prosperity.

The reason is the "Flow of Life" process is more complex than the simple illustrations given earlier.

It also explains why most humans misdirect energy most of the time.

This leads us to the KEY that is vital to the "Total Transformation of our life!"

Chapter 6

Everyone Has Bad Programming

Underlying "garbage" causes all of our challenges

**We are what we think. All that we
are arises with our thoughts.
With our thoughts we make the world.**
the Buddha

Have you ever watched newborn infants? They are like
"little sponges" absorbing information. They observe.
They listen. They continuously collect information
about everything.

This is how we humans come into Classroom Earth.
We are in a state of relative openness. We are open and
receptive to life as it unfolds harmoniously for us and
are constantly and continuously absorbing information
about the world all around us. But because we haven't
yet developed our faculty of discernment, we don't
know the difference between something that is true
verses something that is not true.

In this state of openness, everything we experience and everything we are told is accepted into our "Master Computer" as true.

Our total consciousness is our Master Computer and this includes both our conscious mind and our subconscious mind.

Regardless of whether our experiences (things we are told) are true or false, our "Master Computer" accepts all our experiences and all that we hear into our consciousness. And once the data enters our consciousness, it is all stored in our subconscious mind forever.

Without us being aware of it, all the information and experiences throughout our formative years are stored in our subconscious mind, which I call our Master Computer.

Our acceptance of all data entering our consciousness can create problems for us if the experiences and information are NOT Truth-based. This will continuously create challenges throughout our life experiences.

False data, often called error thoughts, stays in our subconscious mind forever, unless it is consciously removed. All false data is actually Bad Programming. (I also call false data "garbage").

Error thoughts are responsible for most challenges throughout our life!

A term used years ago in computer lingo was "GIGO" which stands for "garbage in… garbage out." If you put "garbage" info into your computer, then "garbage" is going to come out of your computer at various times.

When computers have a glitch, it means something is in the computer that should not be in the computer. This incorrect something ("garbage") causes a glitch in the computer's operation. The "garbage" in the computer continues to adversely affect the computer's effectiveness at a subtle (and sometimes at a NOT So Subtle) level. The "garbage" remains in the computer until it is actively removed.

Much like a computer, we humans have "garbage" stored in our subconscious mind (our Master Computer). And this "garbage" remains in our consciousness, adversely affecting our life in many ways until we actively remove it.

Like a computer, the garbage in our subconscious adversely affects our effectiveness in all life situations, including our goals, our heart's desires, how we interact with others, even the way we deal with our day-to-day plans and activities.

Sometimes the effect is very subtle, maybe not even noticeable at first. But, much like a computer, our effectiveness is compromised by the "garbage" in our subconscious mind, creating a "GLITCH" at various times in life.

The "glitch" might cause us to get unreasonably upset with a co-worker or a loved one. It might show up as an insecurity toward something or someone. It could create a doubt in our mind about our ability to deal with "whatever" situation. It could show up in many different ways.

As it progresses over time, and as more "garbage" is added to our subconscious mind, things happen in our life that might cause us to wonder, "Why is life so difficult?"

The reason life seems difficult at times is because the "garbage" in our subconscious is causing us to experience various "glitches" (challenges). These challenges are really an opportunity to learn and GROW!

Sooner or later the effect of the "garbage" becomes noticeable in our life's journey.

And this is VERY GOOD!

It is good because we cannot fix something if we're unaware that it needs fixing.

The first step toward Self-Mastery is self-awareness!

Being aware of any shortcomings in our consciousness helps us to know we have an OPPORTUNITY to grow!

(If you haven't heard this before, we are all here on Classroom Earth in order to LEARN and GROW!)

Learning and Growing are two entirely different steps!

Learning is the process of getting new data.

Growing means doing something. It means stepping outside of our "habit pattern" (our "comfort zone") and taking a step in a new direction.

We must be willing to change something within us in order to grow.

We cannot grow if nothing changes!!!

Without change, nothing could grow! - not plants, nor animals, nor human beings.

Question: Without change, could life even exist?

Answer: NO! Life could not exist without change. Cells could not split, seeds could not germinate, and nothing could grow.

Bad Programs in our subconscious literally attract the exact challenges to us that we need in order to learn and grow in this situation. This is true regardless of what the situation might be. Challenges are not here to hurt us or to punish us. There are here to help us learn and grow.

We always have the ability to learn and grow!

Whether we choose to learn and grow now, or not learn and grow at present, it is our choice. We always have free will, so we can put off our life lessons however long we choose to put them off to a future date.

However, should we ignore the challenge, we are doomed to repeat it, over and over again, until we are willing to learn our life lesson from the situation, and GROW from the situation. Only then will we stop attracting that situation to our life.

Life really is stacked in our favor.

Sooner or later, no matter how long it takes, we are going to learn our life lessons and grow from them. So eventually we will move into a higher awareness of the Big Picture of life.

What are some of the "Bad Programs" that everyone has in their subconscious mind?

On the following page some examples of "Bad Programming" are listed. These create many of the challenges we humans experience in our lives.

Also listed are a few of the insidious effects that these "garbage" programs have on our belief system.

The "Bad Program"	Ultimate insidious effect on our beliefs
Family business is private business.	Keep secrets. Don't trust non-family people.
You've made your bed, now lie in it.	Mistakes are not allowed. There's no forgiveness.
Blood is thicker than water.	Family loyalty is a "must" whether it is deserved or not.
Don't hang your dirty linen in public.	Don't ask anyone (counselor, minister, etc.) for help. Don't talk about the problem.
Make me proud of you.	You are unimportant until you do something pride-worthy. You've got to EARN mom/dad's love and respect. What you DO is more important that WHO you ARE.

The "Bad Program"	Ultimate insidious effect on our beliefs
Children should be seen and not heard. (also- Don't speak unless spoken to).	You are not even worthy to talk. Everyone else is more important than you. (This fosters unworthiness).
Big boys don't cry.	Don't show emotions even if you're hurting inside. Crying is childish. Crying shows weakness. Men must be strong.
I told you so!	I'm right and you're wrong. Your guidance is better than my guidance. (This foster's self-doubt and feelings of unworthiness).
Money doesn't grow on trees.	There's not enough. (This fosters lack and limited thinking).
You've got to work Hard for money.	Life is hard. It's hard to have "enough."
Don't talk about sex.	Sex is not pure. Our bodies are not pure. There's something wrong with sex and/or something wrong with our bodies.

Recap:

Children come into our world like little "sponges" absorbing all they experience. Regardless of whether experience is true or false (a misperception or misinformation), these experiences (data) are stored in their "Master Computer" (our subconscious mind).

It doesn't matter if the data is TRUE or FALSE, once stored in our subconscious mind, it is treated as truth. The data will remain in our subconscious mind FOREVER, unless we remove it. Until the "garbage" is removed, it will be part of our belief system.

Our belief system affects our TOTAL LIFE EXPERIENCE! It affects how we see life, how we experience life, and how we shape the energy that creates our life experiences.

Chapter 7

Our Individualized Bar Code

You are unique! No other Bar Code is the same as yours.

The two most important days in your life are the day you are born, and the day you find out why.

Mark Twain

An Amazing and Shocking Discovery (The "Bubble" Experience)

A most profound, amazing, and shocking experience happened to me in 1977. This experience forever changed my awareness of us human beings and our human nature.

Shortly after graduating from college, I "discovered" my first metaphysical bookstore.

In my enthusiasm and eagerness to learn, I bought sixteen (16) books!

(Things that delight me or excite me inspire me to jump in with total passion).

Having lived on a tight budget throughout college, working full time each summer and then part-time during the school year in order to support myself and to continue my education, a HUGE interest for me upon graduating from college was to become financially comfortable as soon as possible.

Of the 16 books that I purchased in the metaphysical bookstore, the book I "lived with" was *Open Your Mind To Prosperity* by Catherine Ponder.

On page 32, Catherine stated the importance of doing a forgiveness process every day and included a simple forgiveness prayer. I followed her suggestion and said the short forgiveness process OUT LOUD every day.

It was about five or so lines in length, and although I didn't think I needed to say this every day, for some reason I was drawn to saying it several times each day. It felt good to say this forgiveness prayer.

In saying this forgiveness process several times each day, within a very short time, I had the entire forgiveness process memorized. Several times each day I opened my book to say, out loud, the forgiveness process.

Even though I'd memorized the process, I continued to bring this book home with me each night, and bring it back to my office each morning. I always had the forgiveness process in front of me the many times I'd say it each day.

About two or three weeks into this process of saying this forgiveness prayer out loud several times each day, while sitting at my office desk saying the forgiveness process out loud, a tiny "bubble" at the very pit of my stomach began rising very slowly. It continued to rise ever so slowly, coming up in the center of my body, very gently expanding in size as it continued to rise. It began about half the size of a BB and continued to expand as it slowly came up through my body temple.

I continued saying my forgiveness process out loud while being aware of the sensation of this tiny bubble expanding and rising inside my body. While I didn't know what this bubble was about, I felt safe, comfortable, and relaxed, so I just continued saying my forgiveness process out loud.

The bubble continued to expand and rise, through the center of my chest, my neck, and up through the center of my head. Then it slowly exited through the lower center of my forehead (also known as the "third eye" position).

As the bubble came out of my forehead, it was now a bit larger than a ping pong ball.

The bubble was a pure, white light. Inside the light was a face. As soon as I saw the face, my entire body reacted INSTANTLY! My hands got damp, the hairs on my forearms stood up, and my stomach immediately went into a knot. (See "Psycho-Cybernetics" in the Glossary).

My immediate reaction upon seeing the face inside the bubble made it very clear to me that this was someone I hated as a child. But whatever interaction(s) we had happened so far back in my childhood that I couldn't recall his name. And even more startling, I couldn't remember even one time when we interacted.

My conscious mind had totally blocked out everything that had to do with this person and my subconscious mind wasn't given me any details.

But the overall association stored in my subconscious mind was crystal clear to me.

This person was someone I hated (or at least strongly resented) as a child.

I was totally shocked by this "Bubble Experience."

Always seeing myself as a truly "gentle soul," I didn't think I had any hatred inside of me. Even as a youngster I was a gentle soul who didn't like to fight. And because I just removed myself from incidents where other kids picked on me or made fun of me, I thought that I didn't hold resentments inside of me.

This "Bubble Experience" along with all the physical and emotional feelings that came up with it, made me realize that "Yes, Ron, you hold resentments inside of you."

I immediately saw the humor in my human short-sightedness (and in my human ignorance).

This was a powerful insight into human nature!

I realized that all people hold "garbage" (resentments, hatred, etc.) within their subconscious mind.

Although we might not consciously be aware of it, all our "programming" (both the good and the bad) is always within our consciousness, always affecting our thoughts and feelings. This includes feelings about our self as well as feeling about all others and about life.

This insight had a huge affect on my life. It gave me some early stepping stones into my eventual understanding of the Law of Attraction.

The three valuable lessons I learned through the "Bubble Experience" are:

1- Everyone has "garbage" in their subconscious
2- Regardless of how many years go by, the "garbage" remains in our subconscious. It never goes away by itself.
3- Only the individual can remove "garbage" from their own subconscious mind. A person must consciously choose to remove the "garbage," which can be done through a release process (forgiveness process).

Our Unique Bar Code

There is a Bar Code (UPC code) on every product we purchase. Each product has a unique bar code that, when scanned, not only registers the price of the item, but it also gives data for each item purchased, and thus keeps an accurate, up-to-date inventory on the products that are sold.

The Bar Code and the computer that scans the Bar Code work together doing both the sales and the inventory task, which itemizes the goods needed for the re-ordering process.

Our Master Computer (our subconscious mind) is somewhat like a Bar Code in that it perfectly replicates our total consciousness. Both the conscious and the subconscious mind are components of our total consciousness.

Every Bar Code is totally unique, thus no two Bar Codes could ever be the same. Everything we've ever accepted into our subconscious mind: the good... the bad... and everything in between is always intact within our totally unique Bar Code. This includes ALL the Bad Programming that we've ever experienced or have been told throughout our life.

This Bad Programming in our subconscious mind, "the garbage," adversely affects all areas of our lives: our thoughts, our feelings, our beliefs, and our actions and behaviors.

Everything we've ever experienced... everything we've ever been told as an infant and as a youngster, and most importantly, EVERYTHING WE BELIEVE ABOUT OURSELF, including WHO we are... our self-worth... and more... is all stored in our Master Computer (our subconscious mind).

Our subconscious mind has a complete history of everything an individual has ever heard, as well as everything the individual has ever experienced. Thus our subconscious mind contains a total history of everything an individual has experienced here on Classroom Earth.

The memory banks in our subconscious mind are somewhat like the UPC Code on a product we purchase.

The UPC Code (the Bar Code) is totally unique to each particular product, much like our personal, unique Bar Code within our subconscious mind. Our subconscious mind has stored all of the input we've received since arriving on Classroom Earth.

All of our programming: the good programming... the bad programming... and the everything in between programming... all of it impregnates (shapes) the Unshaped Energy (UE), thus transforming it into Directed Energy (Shaped Energy).

Illustration #6- Our Personal Bar Code
Each person has a unique Bar Code containing true & false information about who they are... how the world is... and the "BIG PICTURE" of life.

Some data in our Bar Code is true... some data is "garbage" (false information, error thoughts, fears, etc.).

The "garbage" (false information) has been accepted into our subconscious mind throughout our life, so our Bar Code contains both GOOD PROGRAMMING and BAD PROGRAMMING. All of it is stored in our subconscious mind.

Perhaps you can recall a time when you or a friend attended a workshop on healing, or prosperity, or on any given topic. You followed all the guidelines and processes, said all the affirmations suggested, and yet did not see a noticeable change in your life.

Why does this happen to so many people?

And not just once, but over and over again?

Illustration #7 explains why this happens to us.

The reason why very little (or nothing) changes in our life after attend a healing workshop, or a prosperity workshop, or "any" workshop is because attendees are only given PART of the needed information to change their consciousness. They only receive part of the information and part of the tools needed to transform one's consciousness. Thus, people are often dealing with only part of the solution, and part of the transformational information.

Most workshops do not cover the Bad Programming in our subconscious mind. Thus, attendees are not given the tools to remove the Bad Programming.

Until we remove the Bad Programming from our subconscious mind, nothing in the "outer" can change because "Life is lived from the inside – out!"

One of the many Scriptural references to this Truth is the verse: "Be it done unto you according to your belief."

What we truly believe (what is programmed in our subconscious mind) is how we "see" life. How we "see" life affects how we respond and/or react to life. It's all about our consciousness. So everything stored in our individual Bar Code is vital to how we experience life.

In the illustration below (Illustration #7), our total consciousness impregnates the Universal (unshaped) Energy... transforming it into Shaped (Directed) Energy by our Total Consciousness. Remember, our Bar Code holds both Good AND Bad Programming and everything in between. All programming goes into the shaping of Universal Energy ➔ transforming it into ➔Directed (shaped) Energy which is then sent out into the universe.

We might be saying affirmations of health and wholeness and are thinking thoughts of health and wholeness in our CONSCIOUS mind, but in our subconscious mind are "garbage" programs of **resentment** toward a person who did "this terrible thing" to me... and our habit pattern of manipulation and/or of undermining other people because we think it helps us get ahead in our job. Other "garbage" programs include hating a group of people because they believe differently than my group... and hating the 'fanatics' in another group because of their violent nature.

The list goes on and on.

While we are doing our affirmation (our prayer) for health and wholeness, our Bar Code is LOADED with resentments and other kinds of "garbage" that is totally out of harmony with LOVE, and thus, totally out of harmony with health and wholeness.

Most of the time most people are praying amiss.

Working with people over many years in spiritual counseling and in just every day conversation, I have many life examples of people misdirecting energy (praying amiss).

In our workshops I do an informal survey asking, "How many people think prayer is answered 100 percent of the time with no Exceptions?"

We usually have about half of the people raise their hand, some add statements like "Prayer is answered in God's time, not necessarily in our time."

After going through the illustrations about our Bar Code and explaining the dynamics of the Law of Attraction, I redo the informal survey. This time almost every hand goes up. Everyone "gets" that prayer is answered 100 percent of the time, with No Exceptions!

Then I give our group the two statements about prayer that I've shared for over twenty-five years.

1 - Prayer is answered 100% of the time with NO EXCEPTIONS!!!

2 - Most people have NO IDEA of what they are praying for.

```
Illustration #7- In addition to our conscious thoughts
(prayers), our entire Bar Code also impregnates the
Universal Energy (Unshaped Energy)… transforming it into
Directed Energy.

If we are praying for healing, but within our Bar Code is
resentment towards anyone… hatred of anyone… envy… etc.,
we are praying amiss!

God is love!  Negative energies are not of love, so they
are not of God.  They are "Out of harmony" with all good,
all wholeness, abundance, etc.

Because negative energies are in our subconscious mind as
Bad Programming, these energies ALSO impregnate the
Universal Energy… go out as part of the Directed Energy…
and return to the sender fulfilled.  This is "praying
amiss."
```

The above illustration is an example of "praying amiss." This happens when we scatter our energy in conflicting directions. We send out both our affirmations of life… AND our Bad Programming of resentment, beliefs that "money doesn't grow on trees," and all the other "garbage" programs.

Scripture clearly tells us, "do not waste our time praying" (about anything) if we have resentment against our brother or sister. Until we release the "garbage" in our subconscious mind, we will always be putting negative energy into our prayers. When our prayers do not come from love, we are praying amiss. We are scattering our energy in all directions, just like a "Light Bulb" (Illustration #1).

Clean out the garbage from our Bar Code! Have our prayer (our energy) be of a Single Focus (like a laser), as in Illustration #2. Then our prayer is empowered!

Once we eliminate the "garbage" from our subconscious, our prayer will be a Single Focus. Then, come back to the altar of your high consciousness and offer your prayer to God / the universe. (Bible reference is Matthew 5:23).

This, dear reader, is effective prayer!

The Bad Programming ("garbage") in our Bar Code remains in our Bar Code FOREVER!

And this "garbage" forever affects our thoughts and feelings about our self and about others. It affects our beliefs about all life areas. (I.e. all that we know and don't know about life, about abundance, about our own self worth, and more).

Our BAR CODE continues to affect our lives forever, until we consciously remove the Bad Programming.

Chapter 8

The Importance of Transforming Our Consciousness

Improving our Life's Experiences (Adding MORE Good to our Life)

Be the change you want to see in the world.
Mahatma Gandhi

Please recall our "Flow of Life" diagram, and that part of every person's Bar Code has some Bad Programming. This Bad Programming has been in our subconscious mind for most of our life here on Classroom Earth.

Knowing this is the first step to correcting the problem.

Self-awareness is the first step toward Self-Mastery!

Being aware that part of our Bar Code contains Bad Programming, we can now understand why, after attending a prosperity workshop (a healing workshop or ANY workshop), and upon using the affirmations suggested, that very little (or nothing) "**seems**" to change in our outer world experience.

This is the experience that many people have after attending workshops because, unknowingly, we still Continue to misdirect energy.

My Dear Friend Vi

More than 20 years ago, Vi retired from her long-time job in South Florida, moved to northern Florida for her retirement years, and we became friends. We often talked about theology as we went to different churches. In several conversations between us, Vi, a widow for more than 10 years, would say that she prays to meet a good man, and to someday get married again.

After hearing this a number of times during our conversations, I finally asked her if she believed that there was someone "for her."

Vi's answer took me by surprise. She said, "NO!"

Knowing how serious Vi is about praying every day, I could hardly believe that she didn't believe in "possibilities"... especially since she knows the power of prayer... and she prays every day.

In my surprise, I asked her, "You don't think that there is anyone "out there" for you, Vi?"

Vi said, "NO! You just don't know what it's like 'out there' Ron. Men 68 years of age don't want a woman who is 68 years of age. They want a woman who is 50 years of age."

I asked, "Do you really believe that?"

Vi answered "Yes!"

So I asked, "Then why do you pray for it to happen?"

Vi said, "I just want to see if God is going to give it to me."

What came out of my mouth was truly "Spirit-Guided" because it just flowed out from me.

I said, "If you pray for a life partner... but in your heart, you truly don't believe there is a life partner for you...' then it is done unto you according to your BELIEF'... not according to your Lip Service."

Vi's prayer was being done unto her according to her *belief.* She truly believed that there was no one "out there" for her because men who are 68'ish didn't want women who are 68'ish, but wanted a woman who is 50 years of age.

This was Vi's belief. Therefore it is Vi's true prayer.

Vi's situation is really true for all people everywhere. It doesn't matter what "lip service" (10 minutes of prayer) we pray. If, in our heart, we have a belief system that is totally opposite of our prayer, then our pray IS answered. Our prayer IS our belief system.

Prayer really is always answered, 100 percent of the time.

Most people just don't know what they are praying for... because most people have no idea of what beliefs are in their subconscious!

Other examples of Bad Programming

Stored within our Bar Code, almost every person alive these Bad Programs: beliefs stating that "Money doesn't grow on trees!"... or that "cancer is bigger than me (stronger than me)"... and many variations of "I'm not worthy."

For example, the belief that "Money doesn't grow on trees!" is often a very long-standing belief system for most people. This is because it has been in our subconscious for so many years, probably since childhood. And because most of us have heard this statement at least a few dozen times from childhood on through the years, many people have had this Bad Program reinforced many times over. This makes it even MORE heavily engrained in the subconscious mind. I call it a **core belief.**

Here's the **GOOD NEWS!**

Every Bad Program in my subconscious mind was inadvertently and unknowingly allowed into my consciousness by ME. I'm the one who allowed it into my consciousness, and I am the only one who can remove it.

This is true for all human beings. All of us have unknowingly allowed Bad Programs ("garbage") into our consciousness, and it is forever stored in our subconscious mind, until we remove it.

Many of us were taught that our challenges in life (health challenges, situation challenges, relationship challenges) are us being punished for things we did, that we shouldn't have done... or for things that we didn't do, that we should have done.

But this is not true. This is a FALSE teaching!

Challenges give us an OPPORTUNITY to learn and to grow. It allows us an opportunity to GROW in a greater awareness of our True Identity.

The Truth is that challenges in our life's journey are never here to hurt us, or to punish us, or even to harm us. Challenges are in our life to help us WAKE UP!!!

"Wake up to what?" one might ask.

The TRUTH about life's challenges is that they are here to help us WAKE UP to our True Identity!

What is our "True Identity?"

Our True Identity is: **"I am a beloved child of God."**

If you're uncomfortable with the word "God"... use "the Divine" instead of the word "God."

Please don't get "lost" over a word!

Do NOT allow ego to take you off course! Ego is so very good at distracting us from the "BIG PICTURE" of life. Please stay focused on the BIG PICTURE!

To keep your awareness on the BIG PICTURE... substitute whatever word you need to substitute for "God." Make it "right" for you.

"I am a beloved child of God!"
... or use...
"I am a beloved child of the Divine!"

I invite you to say this OUT LOUD a few times, pausing for one or two breaths between affirmations to allow the energy of this statement to resonate within you.

"I am a beloved child of God!"

This is my True Identity. This is the True Identity for every person on earth. It is the True Identity for every person who ever lived, and for every person who will ever live.

The word "God" is a name used to mean "The Divine!"... our Higher Self... our Higher Power.

It really doesn't matter what word we use for our Higher Power... it could be God, Great Spirit, Allah, Jehovah, or "whatever." It is just the word we use to identify our HIGHER POWER... the DIVINITY that is always within all of us!

Keep your focus on the Divine! It's in ALL OF US!

Throughout humankind's history, people have argued and have fought thousands of wars over belief systems! Families have been divided over belief systems. Some "lost" family member won't even talk to other family members because of beliefs. And that is so very sad.

Please don't lose sight of the "BIG PICTURE."

Stay with our "BIG PICTURE" FOCUS. **"I am a beloved child of God!"**

This **is our True Identity!**

As we continuously affirm our True Identity, it will seep more deeply into our consciousness. Eventually, we will come to believe our True Identity. And more importantly, we will **LIVE** from the awareness of our True Identity!

But it won't happen overnight, so be persistent in affirming your True Identity several times each day.

Most of us were taught other things about who we are (such as "worms of the dust" and/or "miserable sinners"), so be aware that transformation is a PROCESS. It usually takes time to gradually awaken to our True Identity. Hang in there and continue to affirm your True Identity until you can feel that it is your Truth.

All of us need time to awaken to our True Identity, to bring this awareness into our full consciousness, and to LIVE from this awareness.

This is a typical example of BAD PROGRAMMING. As a youngster, for many years, I was erroneously taught that I'm a "miserable sinner" and a "worm of the dust." Neither of these statements are true about me (or about anyone else). But this is what I was taught, along with hundreds of other children.

It took me YEARS to unlearn this "garbage" because it had been very deeply-rooted into my belief system (and thus, into my subconscious mind).

These false statements were Core Beliefs. They were deeply-rooted because they had been repeated over and over throughout more than a decade during my early, formative years.

But don't worry! We'll soon deal with this "garbage" and all the other "garbage" programs within our Bar Code.

This is just one example of the many Bad Programs that reside within the subconscious minds of people.

So, to help anchor our True Identity into our consciousness, I suggest you do the same thing that I invite all attendees in our workshops to do. I invite you to affirm our True Identity OUT LOUD, several times a day.

This process of transformation rarely happens immediately. Most often, the process of transforming our consciousness happens over time.

Be patient and gentle with ourselves as we move forward in this process.

Stay focused and be aware that you are in the process of transforming our consciousness.

Because you are in the process of transformation, you can also know "The Best is yet to be!"

Chapter 9

Removing "The Garbage"
The True Key of Transformation

When you are offering your gift at the altar, if you remember that your brother or sister has something against you... leave your gift there before the altar, and go... first be reconciled to your brother or sister, and then come and offer your gift.

Matthew 5:23

Removing the "garbage" (the Bad Programming) stored in our subconscious mind is not a very hard task to complete. It's really quite easy. **BUT**, although it is easy, it does require discipline!... and persistence!

The Law of Attraction is the Dynamic that governs everything in the physical universe, from the movement of galaxies... to the movement of sub-atomic particles... and EVERYTHING in between!

There are many sub-laws (sub-topics) that come under the Law of Attraction (also referred to as LOA). One of the sub-laws under the LOA is the Law of Persistence.

The Law of Persistence states: "Whoever (or whatever) persists longest usually wins!"

Please recall my "Most Amazing (and Shocking) Discovery" (see the beginning of Chapter 7).

It was not difficult for me to remove this Bad Program. Even though it was someone I had hated since childhood, please recall that I didn't even know it was inside of me. Also, please recall I didn't have any recollection of any interactions with this individual. This is how very insidious the Bad Programming is throughout our life's journey.

To remove this "garbage" from my subconscious, I merely PERSISTED in saying my forgiveness / release process every day… several times each day. It was actually EFFORTLESS on my part to remove this Bad Program that had been buried in my subconscious mind for decades.

To remove this Bad Program, I only needed to say the Release / Forgiveness Process every day… OUT LOUD!

In using the tool (saying the forgiveness/release process out loud every day), the Bad Program was quickly and easily removed from my Bar Code (from my consciousness).

It merely took Persistence… and discipline to remove this Bad Program. Much more additional "garbage" from my subconscious mind was also removed at the same time. While I don't know any of the other "garbage" that was removed, I do recall feeling very "light" (weight-wise), even though my weight never changed.

MOST of the "Garbage" that was removed from inside of me was removed without my even being aware that it was in my subconscious. To this day, I have no idea of what "garbage" was removed in the release process.

I was only made "aware" of the one major Bad Program because it was Spirit's Way of letting me know something I needed to know in order to help others.

Matthew 5:23 and the Law of Attraction

Please recall the "Flow of Life" Illustration #7 showing how Universal Energy is shaped by our Total Consciousness, which includes both our conscious thoughts AND the Programming (beliefs) of our subconscious mind.

Let's say we are working for a physical healing. We could just as easily be working toward prosperity, or any of our heart's desires. But for this example, we'll use physical healing.

Within our consciousness we have several resentment beliefs. These Bad Programs are "garbage" that affect all of our thoughts. Whether it is a strong hatred for a person who did "that" to me, or however we experienced abuse, or were mistreated, or "whatever" happened… it is an ACTIVE part of our energy field. And it adversely affects all future aspects of our life because it is part of our consciousness.

My affirmation for healing might be: "Thank you God for Your Perfect Life Energy RADIATING throughout every cell of my body temple… renewing and healing me NOW!" But at this exact moment in time, your subconscious mind is also sending out HATRED toward the person who did "it" to you. This scatters our energy (like a light bulb) as our energy goes in opposing directions. This is how people MISDIRECT their personal energy!

Your subconscious hatred toward ANYONE is in direct opposition to HEALING! Healing is *harmony and wholeness. It is a oneness with all good.*

Matthew 5:23 clearly stated this for those "who have eyes to see."

Here is a paraphrase of this verse:

Therefore, if you are there at the altar offering your gifts of healing prayer for your body temple… and you remember you are also sending out resentment/ hatred to your brother or your sister... then STOP WASTING YOUR TIME PRAYING!!! First get rid of the resentment/hatred toward anyone... then come back and offer your PURE prayer to the Universe.

DON'T WASTE TIME PRAYING FOR HEALING!... or prosperity... or a better job... or anything if you are holding hatred and/or resentment in your heart (and your subconscious mind).

Your prayer for healing is ineffective in the above state of consciousness! This is because it is not PURELY about HEALING! It is only PARTLY about healing. AND the energy you are shaping & sending out to the Universe is also is laced with resentment and hatred.

FIRST get rid of the hatred against your brother or your sister...

And THEN come and offer your PURE energy about healing yourself or a loved one.

To clean out the "garbage" in order to go to a Pure Energy (having only Good Programming in our subconscious mind), say both Forgiveness Processes OUT LOUD every day!

THEN come back to the altar (of our consciousness) and offer your gifts in prayer!

The above, stated in the vernacular, is the metaphysics (the higher understanding) of what Jesus was telling us in Matthew 5:23.

Why we must speak 'Out Loud'

We say our Forgiveness and Release process out loud because we are all creatures of habit, and all cells of our body temple 'play to' our habit patterns.

Many years ago Maxwell Matlz wrote a wonderful book called "Psycho-Cybernetics" (see Definition of Terms/Glossary). In his book, Dr. Maltz shared many insightful observations from his work. Following is my paraphrase of one of the most important things I gleaned from his book: "Not only does our mind have memory… but also all the cells in our body have memory[3]."

This was absolutely true in my "Bubble Experience" [shared in Chapter 7] because my entire body reacted INSTANTLY upon seeing "the face" inside the bubble.

Because all cells of our body temple 'play to' our habit patterns, we must CLEARLY AND FIRMLY tell our cells our NEW Standing Orders.

To communicate Most Effectively to all our body's cells, always say The Universal Release OUT LOUD!

All cells of our body temple must clearly hear our "New Standing Orders."

For those who sincerely WANT to improve their lives a bit faster, I suggest saying the forgiveness / release process several times each day as often as you are guided to do so.

In my experience immediately prior to my "Bubble Experience" I was saying a basic forgiveness prayer out loud, several times a day, every day.

Chapter 10

The Universal Release

Total Forgiveness is the path to Unconditional Love and Unconditional Love heals unconditionally.

Ron Palumbo

The Universal Release is an effective, systematic way to remove the Bad Programming (the "garbage") from our subconscious mind. It is a vital gift to our self. Although this gift is totally fFor our self, everyone else also benefits as each person transforms into a higher consciousness (a higher state of awareness).

This very effective tool allows us to forgive OURSELF for any and all error thoughts of the past. It helps us release bad habits we've had in the past. It releases all poor choices from in the past and, most importantly, it eliminates all Bad Programs from our subconscious mind, up to this present moment in time.

TODAY is a new day! From this moment on, always keep our awareness IN THE PRESENT!

To effectively change your consciousness and to "let go of the past" we invite everyone to make a commitment to say the Universal Release OUT LOUD every day.

Say it as many times a day as you are guided to say it, but please consider making a commitment to say it at least once a day as part of your new daily health treatment. It will have a positive affect our mental, emotional, and physical health.

Guidelines for saying the Universal Release

1. During part of your time alone, say the Universal Release out loud.
2. Pause briefly (about two or three relaxed breaths) after each section (at the line spaces between the sections). Allow the words you just stated, to RESONATE within you. Allow your body to "FEEL" the words you are speaking.
3. If something really 'touches you' or, if you feel resistance to any words you've just spoken, take a few moments to re-state these words or phrases, again pausing to allow your body to 'feel' and absorb the energy behind the words.
4. At the first blank space, say YOUR own name.
5. At the second blank space, say whatever comes to mind. It could be something from earlier

today, or from a week ago, or from a decade ago. It doesn't matter "when"… what matters is releasing it.

6. On the third blank space, repeat whatever you stated at the second blank line. (In Step 5 above, you are forgiving yourself for "whatever"… and in Step 6 you are releasing all consequences from "whatever."

7. On the 4th blank space (the last blank space in this section), state the highest thoughts, words, and/or behaviors you can imagine… that will totally transform your previous "unacceptable behavior" (that which you are forgiving yourself for in Steps 5 and 6)… into a behavior that is a blessing to both yourself as well as to all others concerned.

Here's an example of how to use Steps 4, 5, 6, and 7: "Ron, I forgive you for belittling my brother yesterday. I now release all consequences of belittling my brother yesterday and I now honor the Divinity in my brother and treat him respectfully."

Another Example: "Ron, I forgive you for driving like a maniac this morning. I now release all consequences of driving like a maniac this morning, and I now drive safely, honoring all fellow motorists on the highways.

And one more example:

"Ron, I forgive you for <u>eating an entire pizza last night</u>. I now release all consequences of <u>eating an entire pizza last night</u>, and I now <u>honor my body temple and only eat healthy quantities of food</u>.

8. All of us have heart's desires. These are things we'd like to experience or have in our life. It might be a more fulfilling work, or better transportation, or the healing of a fractured relationship, or "whatever."

The next two sections with blank lines are opportunities to put your heart's desires into an Effective Prayer.

An Effective Prayer is a positive affirmation knowing that God not only wants us to live life abundantly, but also that God has already blessed us with all goodness (having already given us dominion over our energy.

Effective Prayer is always stated in the present tense (not "sometime in the future"), and is spoken in gratitude, as if the prayer is already accomplished. It is a realization that the Allness of God's goodness is with us in TOTALITY right now! (This is how Jesus taught us to pray).

Remember, The Universal Release is strictly a gift to our self. It removes Bad Programming from our subconscious mind as it also forgives our self for all errors of the past. It empowers us to more perfectly express the beautiful, Divine being we were created to be... and that we truly already ARE.

Lastly, remember that the Universal Release is an effective tool to let yourself "off the hook" for any of our human shortcomings. It BEGINS the process of removing ALL BAD PROGRAMMING from our subconscious mind.

This usually doesn't happen overnight. So be patient with our self.

This is a process!

Be persistent in your cleansing work... and know the best is yet to be.

"Do the work... and your life improves! There are NO Exceptions!"

The Universal Release

All that has offended me, I forgive. Persons, places, things, I forgive. Within and without, I forgive. Myself and all others, I forgive. Especially myself, I forgive.

I release all condemnation of myself. I release all condemnation of others.

I release all resentment, error thought, and fear. I release poor choices and all behaviors that are not part of the Divine Plan of my life.

I release everyone and everything that are not part of the Divine Plan of my life. Everyone and everything that are not part of the Divine Plan of my life now peacefully release me.

All past errors I release. Consequences of all past errors now release me.

_____, I forgive you for _____.
I release all consequences of _____
and I now_____.

All that has limited me is now released. I am FREE! Thank you God!

I am a pure, perfect channel of love and wisdom. I am clearly guided through this time of awakening... renewal... and transformation. Thank you God!

I am fully awakened to the Divinity within me. I express my Divinity in all that I think, say, and do. Through the Divine Presence in me, I am STRONG and courageous!

I am a beloved child of God... created in God's image and likeness. I am God's perfect channel of love, wisdom, Radiant Life, light, delight, Godservice, laughter and joy, harmony, order, abundance and prosperity, Perfect Health and Wholeness, FUN and BLISS! Thank you, God!

I am _____

In you, O Sweet Spirit, I am _____

New doors of good open before me now. I go forward in my beautiful life's journey. I am a perfect channel of love, wisdom, light, and Truth.

Thank you, God!

Thank you, Dearest Creator!

Thank you, Sweet Spirit.

And so it is!   Amen!

Effectiveness of the Universal Release

I facilitated our empowering 'Law of Attraction' workshop at Unity in Gainesville (FL) in early 1988. One attendee, a newly licensed chiropractic, was dealing with several challenges in life. We begin to **"Do the work"** (say the Universal Release) in our workshop. Attendees are encouraged to continue to release the 'Bad Programming' every day as part of their daily prayer time. Within two weeks, this young man sent a letter to our church, thanking the church members for being part of his Spiritual Family... and for inspiring and supporting him on his life's journey.

A few months later this young man and I again saw each other at an annual conference in Orlando FL. He told me he now works with a husband & wife chiropractic team, and that a portion of his earnings goes toward him becoming a Full Partner in the business. Meanwhile he is **"living in their Very Opulent Home... RENT FREE... until all my debt from Chiropractic School is paid off."**

He then said, "Ron, my life went from the 'pits of hell'... to something out of 'Fantasy Island.' That (The Universal Release) is the MOST POWERFUL THING I've ever experienced IN MY LIFE!"

A Couple Became More Empowered, Saving Both of Their Businesses

A delightful couple attended our 'Law of Attraction' workshop in MN in 2005. Both were very creative, artistic people, each owning their own business. However neither business was thriving… and one business was not bringing in enough income to compensate the owner for his work. The husband was ready to close his business in order to get a job that pays a weekly salary. They begin to **"Do the Work"** in our workshop. Later, we had a counseling session. Within a few weeks of them **"Doing the Work,"** they called my home TWICE in order to record the entire five-verse song they wrote about our "Amazing Workshop"… and how both businesses had an immediate "miraculous" increase in income.

Going from 'Mediocre' Sales… to become The Top Sales Person

Within two months of facilitating our Law of Attraction workshop in Dallas TX, a young woman sent a Thank You letter sharing that she is a health instructor, and they are graded on how many people sign up for the next series of classes. She stated that her sales percentages were always **"mediocre (in the mid-70's). But after attending your workshop and <u>applying</u> the**

techniques, I SKYROCKETED to 98%... and have been in the 90's ever since."

(YES! she actually underlined the word "applying").

But there's more to the story!

Three years later I was a featured speaker at a national healing symposium in Kansas City. After presenting my program, this woman re-introduced herself to me. She told me that after attending our Dallas workshop, she became the TOP SALESPERSON in her INTERNATIONAL COMPANY. And, for being the **"Top Salesperson of the Year,"** she was awarded A NEW CAR.

Chapter 11

The Specific Release

**You have heard that it was said, "You shall
love you neighbor and hate your enemy."
But I say to you, "Love your enemies and
pray for those who persecute you..."**
Matthew 5:43

The Universal Release is an effective tool that, when
used daily, transforms our consciousness by eliminating
all Bad Programming from our subconscious mind. It
is a gift to our self, from our self.

We humans have had challenging experiences with
other people, places, and/or organizations. Except for
spiritually advanced souls, these challenges always
create a negative energy between "me" and one or more
"others" outside of myself.

The Specific Release is an effective tool that, when used
daily, removes ALL NEGATIVE ENERGY between
you and any other person... alive or dead!

When doing the Specific Release, it is best to start
out with the "most challenging" person in your life,

regardless if it was in the past, or is in our present situation. As you remove the negative energy from the "most challenging" life experience (most challenging person), you will feel and be much more empowered. PLUS, releasing all negative energy from other "challenging" persons in the future will be much easier.

The more often you forgive, the easier it becomes. The easier it becomes, the more easily you will forgive. As you continue to do forgiveness work, over time you will find that you are becoming more gentle with yourself and more gentle with your loved ones, and even more gentle with <u>all</u> of God's children.

Guidelines for the Specific Release

1. Say the Specific Release alone (all by yourself).
2. Sit comfortably and calmly in a chair.
3. Visualizing the "other person" sitting calmly in a chair facing you, with your knees almost touching. If this person had traumatized you / victimized you in the past, picture Jesus (or another spiritual master who is meaningful to you) standing at your side, with one hand lovingly on your shoulder, and His other hand lovingly on the "other person's" shoulder.

4. Pause a moment after each statement allowing yourself to FEEL the energy you are sending forth into the Universe. Allow this energy to RESONATE throughout your entire being. If you can't "feel" your words yet,

5. IMAGINE that you DO feel them. Pretend you feel them. Eventually you WILL feel them.

The Specific Release

Throughout the Specific Release, "P N" is the abbreviated version of "Person's Name."

Speaking **OUT LOUD, visualize saying** to the person sitting in the chair:

(P N), I forgive you. I release all negative thoughts and feelings toward you!

(P N), I accept you right where you are in consciousness… and right where you are in life. You are free to unfold to the Divine Plan of your life.

(P N), all things are cleared up between us, now and forever!

(P N), I bless you on your life's journey.

(If person is deceased, use: "(P N), I bless you on your continuing life's journey").

Addressing the Divinity in the other person, say OUT LOUD:

The Divine Presence is now fully awakened throughout (P N)'s entire being now!

(P N), the Divinity in you forgives me and releases all negative thoughts and feelings toward me.

(P N), the Divine Presence in you accepts me right where I am in consciousness... and right where I am in life. The Christ in you frees me to unfold to the Divine Plan of my life.

All things are cleared up between us, now and forever!

(P N), the Divine Presence in you blesses me on my life's journey.

Thank you, God... for your loving presence expressing through (P N), and expressing through me, NOW and forever!

And so it is!   Amen!

(Acid Test)

One question came up often over the early years of facilitating our workshop. It was: "How long do I have to say the Specific Release?"

To answer that question I've added the "Acid Test" to the bottom of this process. The Acid Test is this:

Continue to say the Specific Release out loud, every day until you hold this person in a totally different perspective, with NO negative energy whatsoever. It is a BIG PICTURE perspective.

You'll know when you've arrived in this consciousness of the "BIG PICTURE of life" because you'll then be able to add the word "Dear" in front of this other person's name. You'll Say it! You'll FEEL it! And you'll MEAN it!

When you are able to do this (say "Dear" in front of the person's name, "feel" it, and mean it), you are done saying the Specific Release for this person AT THIS TIME!

At this point you are seeing them as a human being, a beloved child of God, doing their best at any given time, with their various human shortcomings (not knowing any better).

In this consciousness, you are aware that all of us are human beings, doing the best we know how at any given time. At this point, you have finished saying the Specific Release for this person... at this time.

I say "at this time" because next month this person may do something new that again "pushes your buttons." But even if this happens it is almost always easier to forgive a person once you start seeing them as an "unaware" human being, just acting out of ego (the way us humans often do).

As you continue to work with the Universal Release and the Specific Release, you will find yourself becoming

more gentle with yourself.. with your loved ones…
and, eventually, with all others. You'll become more
flexible and accepting of others, and of life situations.
And you will notice that you are more open in more
life situations.

If you have questions about the Universal Release or
the Specific Release, you're welcome to contact me
through my website. If you do contact me, please be
patient as I often have multiple communications after
our 4-Day Healing and Empowerment Series.

You are welcome to sign up for our Law of Attraction
Workshops, our 4-Day Healing and Empowerment Series,
for an individualized or groups "Intensive," and/or for
Counseling Sessions through our website or by email.

At the end of our book there is information on hosting
a "Law of Attraction" Workshop in your area.

Forgiveness Restores Harmony between Mother and Daughter

A California woman shared the effectiveness of the
Specific Release in her life. A wonderful addition to this
story is that she best described the effect of our workshop
succinctly. Upon attending our Law of Attraction
workshop on the Saturday before Thanksgiving, this

woman began the process of removing all negative energy toward any person.

A month later she attended our Christmas Eve Candle Lighting Service. After our service was over, after most people had already left, she shared "her story" with me.

She said that her adult daughter and her had not had even one cfivil (harmonious) phone conversation together in many years. The few times they talked, their conversation degraded into an argument. A few times the anger was so intense that one of them would hang up on the other person. She had been doing the Universal Release every day for her daughter and added, "Out of the blue, her daughter called her about a week or so after the workshop. Our phone conversation was SO GOOD that we decided we would have lunch together the following week. And depending on how lunch went… we "might" do a little Christmas shopping together."

She said, "It was like two life-long friends had been reunited after many years apart. We laughed… we giggled… we held hands… we had a BLAST!"

Then she said, **"Ron, if I hadn't taken your workshop, I would have called this a miracle! But BECAUSE I took your workshop, I kind-a thought something like this might happen."**

From a Lawsuit Threat... Back to Harmony and Cooperation

A successful business woman attended our Law of Attraction workshop in a large city one Sunday, thus began to **"Do the Work."** Monday night she attended Part 2 of our workshop and shared her AMAZING EXPERIENCE with our group. She said she had lent a large sum of money to her "at that time boyfriend" a while back. Because they had a wonderful relationship at that time, she didn't have him sign a Promissory Note. She had nothing in writing.

After they broke up, a month or so later when she asked about getting repaid her for her loan, he got upset and their friendship drastically deteriorated from that point on. Saturday, the day before our workshop, he told her he was going to have his 'high-priced lawyer' harass her continuously. She hung up on him and said she would not take any more of his phone calls. The next day she attended our workshop and began the process of releasing ALL negative energy between her and this man. The next morning he called her office and told this woman's secretary that he didn't want to fight with her anymore... and that he would begin making payments to her until the entire loan was paid in full.

A Father and Daughter Reunited

In September of 2013, a successful business woman attended our 4-Day Healing & Empowerment Series in Montana. We always begin our series with our 4-Hour Law of Attraction Workshop, thus she began to **"Do the Work."**

Prior to our workshop, this woman had shared that she and her father used to be very close while she was growing up, but after becoming an adult and her becoming a business woman herself... she and her father had a disagreement ... and that they had not talked nor visited each other very much over several years.

Five days after leaving Montana, this woman sent me an email saying that her father had called her... and they talked for an hour or so... and that while he never apologized to her, he did tell her he was "very proud" of her.

Releasing 'the Hurt' and the 'Heavy Weight' on her Shoulder

A woman in New York 'seemed to' be **"Doing the Work"** in our Sunday workshop. The next day, while having coffee in her kitchen, I asked if she did the

Specific Release this morning (for her relationship with her brother).

She said she "couldn't do it" because he had done horrific things, including trying to have her committed in an institution.

We then had (what I call) a "Prayer Meeting." This is a strong disagreement where I have to "tell it like it is! I continuously told her she must release the negative energy in order **for HER to be free**. I added that it has nothing to do with her brother. Holding extreme resentment harms the HOLDER of the resentment. It doesn't harm the person you resent. Resentment adversely affects the health of the person HOLDING the resentment, but has no effect on the health of the person being resented. After about 15 minutes of me adamantly "telling it like it is"… she finally agreed to say the Specific Release. I left her kitchen to give her space to **"Do the Work."** I went into the living room to check my email messages. One email message was from the woman in Montana. (Her story is just above this one).

I laughed out loud.

About two minutes later, the NY woman came into the living room almost yelling, **"I can't believe how good I feel. It's like a HUGE weight has been lifted off my shoulders."**

Chapter 12

Chemicalization

**Lead me from the unreal to the real;
lead me from darkness to light**

from the Upanishad

Recall a time when you cleaned out a garage, an attic, a basement, or anything that has been stagnant for years. About a half-hour into the project, what did the area around the garage (attic or basement) look like?

It was a TOTAL MESS!

We previously mentioned that life is lived from the "Inside – Out" - which was explained in detail through our Flow of Life illustrations and information.

Because life is lived from the "Inside-Out," as we utilize the Universal Release technique and the Specific Release technique every day, we are continuously removing Bad Programming in our subconscious. We are also eliminating all Negative Energy between our self and any other person… alive or dead.

In doing so, we are putting our entire consciousness in a state of flux (a state of transformation).

Because life is lived from the Inside – Out, what do you suppose our "outer world" might look like when our entire consciousness is undergoing a MAJOR transformation?

Our "outer world" **MIGHT** (temporarily) look like a MESS!!!

(Much like our attic cleaning project would look as we start removing the 'stuff' after years of neglect).

While this doesn't happen to everyone, some folks do experience what seems like, "everything is falling apart."

Should your world seem to be falling apart, don't panic!!!

First of all, CONGRATULATE yourself!

You are experiencing the effects of your transformation of consciousness!

This is GREAT!!!

Next, realize that what you are experiencing is much like looking at the overall effect of what cleaning out the garage might look like after being part of the way into the project.

Do you stop cleaning out the garage because it looks like a mess???

NO! You push forward to complete the work!

This is the same thing we must do if it seems like things in our world are falling apart.

It is NOT falling apart! What is happening is that you are releasing "stuff" that is no longer part of the Divine Plan of your life.

LET IT GO!!!

It no longer serves you!

You are opening yourself to a higher level of life because you are eliminating the "garbage" (error thoughts, false beliefs, etc.) that has been holding you back your entire life.

The best thing to do in this situation is to push forward with ***more intensity and more enthusiasm!***

Say your Universal Release SEVERAL MORE TIMES each day!

It's your life! How quickly would you like to improve your life's experiences?

Chapter 13

Anger

Don't let ego run your life
– Ron Palumbo

Let's address anger. Is it good? Or is anger bad?

Anger, of itself, is not bad. Anger is merely an internal experience letting us know that something really upsets us. The situation that upsets us 'triggers' our emotional nature.

In reality, anger is an internal gage making us aware of something that doesn't work for us BIG TIME!

How we deal with anger is what makes it either healthy or unhealthy.

We can channel our anger in one of two ways. We can channel our energy in a constructive way, or in a destructive way. It is always our choice.

To channel anger in a Constructive Way, there are only two rules:

- We cannot hurt our self
- We cannot hurt anyone else

Next, to resolve the anger (move **through** the anger bringing our emotional nature back to an even keel), the two rules to complete the constructive resolution of the situation are:

- We have to "Feel" our feelings
- We have to "express" our feelings

In expressing our feelings, remember we cannot hurt our self and we cannot hurt anyone else.

There's an important aspect of anger to be aware of in order to resolve it so that we can "get on" with our life.

If we are really upset by "whatever" and are feeling a very high level of anger, and especially if we are feeling powerless in a particular situation, we still must move through the anger in order to return to balance in our life.

Also, we must move through the anger in order to do our forgiveness work.

But when our emotions are in a very high level of 'upset,' and our stomach is "tied in a knot," as hard as we may 'try' to do our forgiveness work, we will not be able to do it effectively.

We can never do our forgiveness work in the above setting. First we must 'feel' our feelings.

Then we must 'express' our feelings!

After we allow ourselves to feel our feelings, and then express our feelings (without hurting our self or anyone else), only then can we *effectively* do our forgiveness process.

The emotional hold that intense anger creates cannot be bypassed until we resolve the "anger energy" within us!

I'm speaking from experience because another wonderful Life Lesson fell into my lap. It didn't feel like a lesson at the time because it was very painful both physically and emotionally.

(Do life lessons ever feel like lessons in the heat of the moment?)

Many years ago I was in a post-graduate program where the instructor had some very serious unresolved issues. This instructor was intentionally doing several dysfunctional and unethical behaviors toward me and several other students in this particular class.

Having taught forgiveness in LOA workshops for over ten years prior to this time, I knew I had to forgive this person. But every time I went through the entire forgiveness process, it never "took."

I never 'felt' the forgiveness words that I was saying out loud.

My words were powerless and I knew it!

Then one night while alone in my home, out of a total frustration over this unfair and very unethical situation… plus my additional frustration over not being able to effectively do the forgiveness work that was so desperately needed… I began to rant and rave… yelling out my frustrations toward this dysfunctional person. (Remember I was alone, so I was the only person to hear my words).

I ranted and raved about the unfairness of the situation, "blasted her unethical behavior" up one side and down the other side, and just carried on like I'd never done before (or since).

This went on for quite some time. I totally "let my hair down" that evening telling this instructor what a jerk she was, how unfair and unethical she was, etc. I let it all out.

After about a half-hour of my ranting and raving and cussing her out, I felt like a wet noodle. There was nothing left inside of me.

My stomach was no longer "in a knot" and I was no longer a raving maniac. It was all 'gone.'

Realizing that I had moved through a HUGE barrier, I then began my Specific Release out loud.

This time (for the first time for this person and this situation) the Specific Release finally "clicked."

I felt the power of my words!

I was able to release all the negative energy between this person and myself that very night.

Did our relationship change? You bet it did!

She was still dysfunctional and unethical, however, she was no longer so focused on me. Also, she no longer "ruffled my feathers." I just accepted here right where she was in consciousness.

While my situation was completely unknown to anyone, this instructor had other 'discrepancies' come to the attention of the Dean of Education by the end of the semester. She was released from her teaching position.

My Life Lesson from this experience

I was blessed to learn all the rules for moving through anger in a constructive way.

There are dozens of ways to express anger without hurting anyone.

The way it worked for me in the above situation was part of my learning curve. But having learned the lesson from that situation, I wouldn't have to do ranting and raving ever again.

Generally, express your feelings by yourself, in private however it feels 'right' to you.

There might be certain situations where another person is experiencing the same frustration and the same anger. In this situation you might have a shared time of expressing your feelings.

Just remember you cannot hurt yourselves and you cannot hurt anyone else.

Here are just a few examples of ways to express anger constructively:

- While driving by yourself, especially in the open country, shout out your feelings
- Say/shout whatever you need to say/shout while punching a pillow
- Say/shout "whatever" while doing any intense physical activity (i.e. slamming a tennis ball into a racket ball court, intense swimming, running, most intense physical activities).

After working with the Specific Release processes for a while, you'll come to have more gentle ways to express your feelings.

Some of these "more gentle" ways might include:

- Writing a letter to the other person.
- NEVER MAIL THE LETTER!!!
- This is vital, so I repeat: NEVER MAIL THE LETTER!!!
- Write "whatever" in your journal
- Share "whatever" with your spiritual mentor
- Share "whatever" with a close friend who will keep it a secret!

As we continue using the forgiveness processes in this book, we'll come to a place in our lives where it will become more and more difficult for us to feel an intense anger. We will find ourselves being more compassionate toward our self and with all other. We will become more forgiving and more honoring of all of God's children.

It's all part of our learning and growing process. And it is all part of our transformation.

Chapter 14

An Effective Stress-Relieving Technique

"Choose this day whom you will serve..."
Joshua 24:15

At any time, in any situation, we can utilize our dominion by choosing to focus our energy to relax our body temple, and thus eliminate or reduce stress. This would be using our dominion WISELY.

The following stress-relieving technique is always available to us, even if we have to go to the restroom in order to have a few moments alone in order to focus our energy.

- Breathe deeply! Take a deep inhalation and hold this breath for 7 or more seconds. Then gently and slowly exhale.
- Affirm: **"The Perfect Peace of God is within me."** Pause and take about 4 normal, relaxed breathes.
- Take a second deep breath, following the same process as above.

- Affirm: **"I completely relax in God's Perfect Peace."** Pause and take about 4 normal, relaxed breathes.
- Take a third deep breath, again following the same process above.
- Affirm: **"I am the calm, poised, relaxed, beloved child of God."** Pause for 4 normal, relaxed breathes.
- "Feel" the peace of God within you. Allow yourself to completely relax in God's Perfect Peace. Allow yourself to take about 10 relaxed, normal breathes.
- Affirm: **"God is with me therefore nothing can disturb the calm peace of my soul."**
- After a few minutes of relaxation, take a gentle deeper breath, bringing yourself back to this present moment in time. Take one more deep breathe and as you exhale, affirm: **"Thank you God for your Perfect Peace within me."**

* Several times throughout the day, take three deep breathes as per the first step.

Chapter 15

Accelerating Our Empowerment

You shall know the Truth, and the Truth shall set you free.

John 8:32

We are created to be empowered beings.

If we refer back to the wisdom teachings (the mystical teachings) of Scripture, God created humankind in God's own image and likeness. He then gave humankind DOMINION over the fish of the sea (our deepest feelings/ our subconscious mind), and over the birds of the air (our highest, inspirational thoughts), and over the cattle (our habit patterns and our animal nature), and over all the wild animals of the earth (our ego and our appetites) – Genesis 1:26

"God saw everything that He had made and, indeed, it was VERY GOOD" – Gen.1:31

So when God / the Divine / the Universe Source created us, we were given dominion over everything.

The 'everything' that we have dominion over is our own personal energy!

By our personal energy, we are continuously co-creating the physical world that we are experiencing.

All of us continuously shape energy, direct energy, and much of the time, we mainly misdirect energy.

However we use the Law of Attraction, for good or for chaos, we are always creating our worldly experiences.

Use the Law of Attraction WISELY and it will help us to learn and grow. It will help us to move into a higher level of empowerment because it will accelerate our transformation process.

Following are some of the ways to further accelerate our empowerment process.

Accelerating our Empowerment process:

- **Remove all Bad Programming from our subconscious mind.** Say the Universal Release out loud every day. Soon you'll feel a wonderful shift of consciousness has taken place. You'll feel better about yourself. You'll feel better about life. You'll treat yourself more lovingly. And you'll be treating your loved ones and all others more lovingly.

- **Release ALL Negative Energy between you and any other person... alive or dead.** Say the Specific Release out loud every day. Continue to say this for any given person until there is NO Negative Energy left within you. This means there is NO emotional charge when you see this person or when you think of this person or when someone mentions this person's name). Continue saying the Specific Release until you can pass Ron's Acid Test. (As you say the Specific Release, you can say "Dear" in front of this person's name every time you speak the name in your Specific Release. You say "Dear" and you can "feel" it. You truly 'feel' the words because you mean it!) Once you pass this 'Acid Test' you no longer have to say the Specific Release for this person at this time.

- **Know who you ARE!** We are all created in the image and likeness of the Divine, and we all have Divinity within us. Affirm your True Identity several times throughout the day. Everyone's True Identity is: **"I am a beautiful, beloved child of God."**

- **Speak words of gratitude every morning.** My favorite morning affirmation is: "Thank you God for this beautiful... MARVELOUS... glorious day!" It is then followed with "thank you God" for "whatever" other items that come to mind.

Speak words of gratitude and appreciation throughout the day, every day.

- **Relax in the silence every day.** Meditation is one of the best healing processes known to humankind (or at least known to "some" humans). Several medical doctors have acknowledged that our body heals itself when it is taken out of stress for a sufficient period of time. Meditation allows our body to deeply relax and HEAL.
- **Use our (or any) Stress-Relieving Technique as needed.** Not only does our body heal itself when taken out of stress… but also we work better, think better, are more creative, etc.

Chapter 16

S-L-O-W-I-N-G the Aging Process

"I'm ageless and timeless"
– Peace Pilgrim

"My age is none of my business"
– Eric Butterworth

The biggest factors affecting our aging process is usually not our genes. More often than not, our biggest factors are:

- How well we live our life
- The energy of our thoughts about health and wholeness
- The words we put out to the universe
- How well we are 'open' to the flow of life energy to renew and rejuvenate our body's cells

Several studies show that we decrease our risk of stroke by 50% by doing four things:

1. Be active for 30 minutes a day, at least four days a week

2. Eat five daily servings of fruits and vegetables
3. Avoid the use of tobacco products, including second-hand smoke
4. Avoid using excessive alcohol

While most of the above seem to be common sense, there are additional steps we can take to Effectively S-L-O-W our aging process.

Ways to effectively S-L-O-W the aging process include:

1. **Reduce stress** – Our body naturally renews and heals itself as we reduce stress. (Remember, simple deep breathing reduces stress).
2. **Meditate daily** – Meditation eliminates stress in our body and helps us be more centered in our daily activities.
3. **Use life-affirming affirmations daily** – Bless your body daily. Affirm perfect life energy flowing throughout your body, and especially to any areas that need to be renewed and healed.
4. **Exercise regularly** – Regular exercise 4 times a week keeps your life energy flowing throughout your body. If nothing else, a brisk walk several times a week is GREAT exercise.
5. **Drink plenty of water** – Keeping your body hydrated is very important to your overall health.

6. **Eliminate soft drinks and all carbonated beverages as much as possible.**

7. **Get off the "Age Merry-Go-Round"** – STOP focusing on your age. And stop focusing on the age of other people. The age of other people is none of your business. You are a spiritual being therefore you are "ageless and timeless." That is the truth of who you are!

8. **Eat balanced, nutritious meals** – Eliminate fast foods and processed foods as much as possible. Eliminate or drastically reduce sodium as much as possible. If you use salt at all, use Sea Salt. Eliminate (or highly dilute) high fructose corn syrup beverages, and use sugar sparingly. Eat lots of fruits and vegetables and foods that are close to their natural state (not too heavily processed).

9. **Maintain good hygiene** – Good hygiene supports your body's longevity.

10. **Hydrate your skin daily with a good moisturizer** – This is especially important for people living in a dryer climate.

11. **Avoid too much direct sunlight** – Not only does too much direct sunlight dry and age our skin, but excessive sunlight can also damage our skin.

12. **Floss every day** – Daily flossing reduces the amount of gum-disease-causing bacteria in the mouth.

13. **Keep moving** – Stay active. One doctor states that exercise is the only real Fountain of Youth.

14. **Get at least 6 hours of sleep each day** – Sleep is how our body renews and heals itself.

15. **Stay connected to friends and loved ones** – It not only helps to keep your life in balance, but also you are part of a team that is available when one or the other needs help.

Chapter 17

Attitudes that foster a Happy, Successful, Prosperous Life

"What you think, you become"

– Mahatma Gandhi

Many years ago, at the conclusion of my first New Thought Retreat, all attendees were given an evaluation form to give our feedback about various aspects of our weekend retreat.

One of the categories was: "What topics/classes would you like to see at next year's retreat?"

Aware of how important "Attitude" is in our life's journey and how it affects everything we experience in life, I wrote "Attitude: The Key to Success In Life."

Next year, I again attended this weekend retreat. but there were no presentations on the topic of "Attitude."

But, again, at the conclusion of the retreat, once again we were given Evaluation Forms to be filled out and turned in before leaving the retreat grounds.

Again, I suggested, "A Positive Attitude Makes Life More Enjoyable."

The following year, again, no class or presentation on "Attitude." So once again, (for e third consecutive year) on my Evaluation Form, I again suggested/requested a class on "Attitude."

Upon arriving for my fourth (4th) consecutive retreat, and again discovering that none of our weekend instructors/ministers were doing a class on "attitude" a voice from within me said, "If you want a class on 'Attitude,' Ron, guess who's going to lead the class?"

And I "Knew" the answer.

I was going to be the one to teach a class on attitude.

Eventually I did teach this class, many times over.

Years later, while taking private pilot lessons, the control panel instrument that seemed to "leap out at me" was the "Attitude Indicator."

By looking at this gage, you could immediately tell if the plane was flying level, or if it was losing altitude (going down), or if it was climbing (going up).

I LOVED the Attitude Indicator!

I immediately thought, "If people could have an Attitude Indicator strapped to their wrist like a watch, they would always be able to tell if they were on an even keel, or if their attitude was taking them "down," or if their attitude was allowing them to "go higher" (rise in consciousness).

A true fact of life is that our attitude truly 'flavors' how well we will enjoy our life's journey here on Classroom Earth.

Our attitude is a major ley that fosters living a happy, successful, and prosperous life.

A Few Key Attitudes that foster a well-lived life

1. **An Attitude of Gratitude** is one of the most life-enhancing attitudes we can foster. It is one of the most important attitudes we can have. It is also one of the most rewarded attitudes in life.

   Gratitude literally amplifies (increases) the energy we send out to the universe, to which the universe then sends back to us fulfilled.
   (Please recall or review Chapter 5 - "The Flow of Life").

2. **An Attitude of Trust.** As we become more aware of our True Identity, we will awaken to the Truth that the Divine is always within us, always guiding us, and always wanting the very best for us. We will become more open and more flexible with all of life. This includes any "bumps" that might come up in our life's journey.

3. **An Attitude of Awareness.** Throughout the day we have many thoughts that come across our mind. Know that Divine thoughts /good thoughts bring good into our life. Thoughts that entertain willfulness, obsessions, manipulations, controlling others, greed-based thoughts are all ego-based thoughts. These are NOT worthy of our attention. Choose to entertain only good thoughts.

If we are challenged to get out of "ego-based" idol thinking, think about a friend who is a blessing in our life and then send a blessing to this friend. Sending a blessing to a friend is as simple as saying, "God bless you, Dear Tony."

A Scripture verse from Philippians 4:8 states: "Whatever is just… whatever is pure… whatever is pleasing… whatever is commendable, if there is any excellence and anything worthy of praise, think about these things.

4. **An Attitude of Service.** People who serve others out of love, not from any work-related situation, are some of the happiest people on earth. To inspire another human being, to encourage another, to be there for a friend in a time of need, these are just a few of the many ways we can serve others. Each act of service that comes from love blesses both the giver of the service AND the receiver of the service. Service is literally an act of love.

5. **An Attitude of Openness and Flexibility.** Throughout out life's journey there will be many changes that happen. Change is inevitable. Life could not exist without change. Resistance to change is foolish. All pain and suffering that comes from resistance to change is OPTIONAL PAIN.

In realizing that life will constantly change, it is wise to be OPEN to change and to look for the good in the change.

Remember: everything that is visible is temporary! We are only visitors here on Classroom Earth.

Being open to life and be flexible with life. This will make your life's journey much more enjoyable.

Glossary

Terms Used in this Book

Affirm – to declare a Truth. Truth Affirmations are positive statements, stated in the present tense. Truth Affirmations are made with an awareness that the "allness of God" is everywhere present at all times, including within us and all around us. God is always present in all situations.

Affirm comes from the Latin word "affirmare" which means "to strengthen."

Anger – an internal reaction or response to someone or something that 'triggers' our emotions (pushes our buttons). Of itself, anger is neither good nor bad. But depending on whether we 'react' to the person or situation, or if we 'respond' to the person or situation, we make the result of anger good or bad. How we choose to *deal with the anger* is what makes it good or bad. (See "respond" and "react" below).

Awareness – is the ability to perceive; the capacity to have knowledge of.

Bar Code – the illustration this author has been using to represent the Good and Bad Programming that is accepted into (and forever stored within) the memory banks of our subconscious mind. Just as each product has its own Bar Code, so too each human being has their own individual Bar Code.

This illustration has been a very effective tool, giving workshop attendees a visual description of the dynamic process of the Law of Attraction.

Being – the state of existence. We are both human beings as well as spiritual beings. Our human "earth suit" is temporary, as we are all just visiting "Classroom Earth." We are spiritual beings, and we will always be spiritual beings even after we leave "Classroom Earth."

Bible – the most mystical, insightful book ever written. To get the higher teachings of Scripture, it must be studied and understood metaphysically. (Jesus often spoke in metaphysical language and terms, and his analogies were almost always metaphysical.

To better understand the Bible, one must be aware of the people who wrote the Bible, their ancient culture and their ancient customs. One must also understand what was both accepted and understood in the writings of that time, the customs as a people including their use of exaggeration, symbology, (especially the symbology of numbers and names).

The Bible is literally the story of every person's personal journey through Classroom Earth, growing from ignorance into fully responsible, empowered, fully awakened children of the Divine.

When understood metaphysically, it is the most amazing, insightful, and mystical book ever written.

BIG PICTURE / Big Picture of Life – an awareness of our spiritual identity and the relationship we have with the Divine, with each other, and with all of life. It is an ability to see any given situation from a higher awareness that goes beyond the immediate situation.

Bliss – pure, ultimate joy. Bliss is often times experienced when we are in a state of deep meditation (a state of timelessness).

Classroom Earth – The author sees planet Earth as a classroom. Everyone is here to learn and grow. This is true for all humans, whether we know it or not. We are all created in the image and likeness of the Divine. And no matter what else we choose to do with our life, the bottom line is that we're here to **"Wake Up to our Divinity!"** Everything else that we do is secondary to our main purpose for being here on Classroom Earth.

The author uses the term "Classroom Earth" because it is where we are getting this phase of our education about our True Identity. He considers Classroom Earth about Third Grade Level of our learning and growing (awakening) process. This opinion of the author is based on the insanity that goes on throughout our planet.

Conscious mind – holds knowledge of the items that we are aware of, such as things we know and thoughts we are aware of.

Consciousness – is all three levels of awareness, including the conscious mind... the subconscious mind... and the super conscious (Divine) mind.

Core Belief – a long standing belief in our subconscious mind, which has been reinforced dozens of times over the years. A Core Belief can be either a good or a bad program in our subconscious.

Ego – comes into the world much like an untrained puppy. The ego, of itself, is not bad. It is merely untrained. If left untrained, it can become a tyrant in our life because an untrained ego literally "wants what it wants when it wants it, and it always wants it NOW." In this case, ego stands for Edging God Out. However, when the ego is lovingly taught with firmness and wisdom, it serves us very well. In part, it gives us our identity of our physical self and the determination to "go for 'whatever' goal is before us." The ego is partly our connection to the physical world.

Egomaniac – an exaggerated belief that one is far better than anyone else and more important than anyone else. It is often characterized by an obnoxious arrogance and a strong willfulness that things have to be done "my way!"

Error thought – a false belief. When presented with error thought, if we do not reject it as untrue, the error thought goes into (and is stored) in our subconscious mind forever, unless it is removed.

Evolution – the gradual process of change where all life forms adapt to their environment and/or to new knowledge / new awareness. For human beings, this also includes learning and growing we well as becoming self-actualized (fully awakened).

Faith – often used in a religious or a spiritual connotation, but also includes a belief in another person. It is a belief without having physical evidence or proof, a belief in things unseen.

Flow of Life – the dynamic process that governs everything in the physical universe, from the movement of galaxies down to the movement of sub-atomic particles, and everything in between.

It includes the shaping and directing of Universal Energy, transforming it into Directed Energy where it then goes out "to the universe" and is ultimately returned to the sender of the energy, fulfilled.

Universal substance (Unshaped, Universal Energy) is present everywhere throughout the universe. It is unshaped and undirected (neutral) substance. Thoughts shape universal substance, thus transform it into Directed Energy.

Directed Energy is energy that has been shaped by one's thoughts. Once shaped, this energy goes out into the universe. The universe always says "YES!" to shaped (Directed) energy, then returns to the sender of the energy, fulfilled (manifested as identical energy to the original energy sent out).

The universe always accepts Directed Energy and then returns said energy back to the sender fulfilled. This is how we humans manifest (co-create) our life's experiences.

"As you sow, so shall you reap" is one of the many descriptions for this all-encompassing dynamic. Other names and/or descriptions include karma, what goes around comes around, the circle of life, and other names/descriptions as well. All descriptions, including the Flow of Life, are governed by the Law of Attraction.

God – the Ultimate Reality. The many different paths (faiths) use many different names for this Ultimate Reality, including the Divine, Jehovah, Great Spirit, the Buddah, Lord, Pure Reality, God, Divine Presence, the Allness, Allah, the ISNESS, etc.

The best definition of God is LOVE… pure, unconditional LOVE!

A verse of Sacred Scripture clearly states, "… Love one another because love is from God; everyone who loves is born of God and knows God. Whoever does not love does not know God, for God is love" (1 John 4:7).

Unconditional Love is the True, Pure Essence of the Divine.

Grace – a positive energy that is always blessing us. This author believes this is part of the reason that we continuously awaken to higher states of awareness, and why all life continuously grows and evolves.

Heal / healing – to make whole and complete. We can be healed because, spiritually, we are created in the image and likeness of God… whole, perfect, and complete.

Heaven – from the ancient Aramaic, literally means "expanding consciousness."

Much later, this concept was mistranslated into being "a place in the cosmos, where the Divine Presence resides," far above the earth, somewhat removed from the earth.

Intuition – the ability to perceive or discern the innate wisdom that is within us, above and beyond our "intellect." It is a guidance that comes from our Higher Power… the Divine Presence within us.

Karma – a term similar to, but with some variation to the Law of Cause and Effect. Karma, which is Old Testament thinking, does not accept the concept of forgiveness. The Old Testament teaches "an eye for an eye and a tooth for a tooth." This Old Testament thinking was transformed by Jesus when He introduced the concept of forgiveness. Throughout His ministry He encouraged people to practice forgiveness unceasingly! (Seventy times seven).

Law of Attraction – the dynamic that governs everything in the physical universe from the movement of galaxies down to the movement of sub-atomic particles and everything in between.

The Law of Attraction has been known by many names and phrases, such as the Law of Cause and Effect, Karma, "As you sow, so shall you reap," and the very similar, "Be it done unto you according to your faith," and a few other phrases.

Law of Cause and Effect – see the Law of Attraction (above)

Meditation – a relaxation process that shifts our awareness from the "outer world" thoughts and activities, to the Divine Presence within. It is a place of peaceful stillness. As we go into a state of deep relaxation, we are stress-free. In this state of comfort, out body's cells are able to do what they were designed to do. They are renewed and rejuvenated by the life energy flowing through them.

Life energy is always available to us, but stress literally blocks the life energy from us. Meditation eliminates stress, which is why meditation has been known to be a powerful healing practice.

In addition to helping the healing practice, meditation has dozens of other healthy benefits.

Metaphysics – from two ancient Greek words: "meta" and "physica."

Meta = beyond or underlying, and physica = the physical or the physics.

So metaphysical means "beyond the physical"… or "that which underlies the physical."

Many of the words and sayings attributed to Jesus were metaphysical in nature.

Miracle – an event that occurs outside the "KNOWN" laws of nature.

My guru, Eric Butterworth often stated, "There are NO miracles!"

Although I strongly disagreed with him back in the late 1970's, over time I came to realize that Eric is correct. There are NO miracles.

Charles Fillmore, an American Mystic during the early and mid 1900's stated, "Miraculous events are not outside the laws of nature but are a HIGHER understanding OF the Laws of Nature. They are first, an awareness of the allness of God in 'this' very situation, and then a calling forth of God's unlimited good in 'this' situation!"

This is EXACTLY how Jesus did His "miracles!" He always saw the Allness of God in the very midst of "whatever" situation and He called forth God's goodness. Lastly, He ALWAYS gave thanks to God BEFORE the "miracle" was complete. He "prayed as if it was already 'done'."

Jesus prayed using Effective Prayer!

Mystic – one who is aware of the Divine Presence throughout the day and sees the Divine in most (or all) situations.

New Thought – a spiritual path that acknowledges God's Presence in all people, thus ALL people are beloved children of God. New Thought goes back to the PURE teaching of Jesus BEFORE any man-made doctrine or dogma was added to His teachings.

"Psycho-Cybernetics" – an insightful book by Dr. Maxwell Maltz. In it, he shared his discovery that not only does our mind have memory, but also all the cells of our body temple have memory as well.

Dr. Maltz's book included several other insightful discoveries as well.

Psychometry – discerning the energy field of a person or of an object belonging to a person (i.e. their car keys, wallet, cosmetic case, etc.).

Psychometry includes the ability to "perceive the energy" of a person, an object, or a group. While this ability is within everyone, most people do not utilize the have this ability. They are unaware that this is a God-given ability within them. Therefore, most folks never develop this ability within them.

React – dealing with a situation at a level of a 'knee jerk reaction.' It is not coming from a place of being 'centered,' or of an awareness of the "Big Picture of Life." It is merely a 'reaction' to a situation outside of our self. It is usually ego-based (fear-based). This is very different from 'responding' to an outer situation. (See 'Respond' below).

Respond – dealing with a person or situation from an awareness of the 'Big Picture' of life. It is being 'centered' while dealing with the situation. This is very different from "reacting" to an outer situation. (See 'React' above).

Technique – a systematic process that effectively produces a desired result.

Upanishad – part of the Sacred Scripture that was written in Sanskrit, an ancient language used by the Hindus in India almost 3,000 years ago. It mainly consists of a truth student asking questions to his mentor/teacher and the responses his mentor/teacher gives to the student.

Visualize - to hold a concept or thought in one's mind. This engages our faculty of imagination.

To "see" a thing or an outcome in our mind's eye. This is also called, "Holding the High Watch."

Endnotes

1. There is always a slight positive (friendly) charge in all energy, including the Unshaped Universal Energy.

    The author believes this slight positive charge is present in the Unshaped Universal Energy because the Source of all energy is the Divine (God / our Higher Power).

    This belief is another way of restating Einstein's words: "We live in a friendly universe."

2. We GREATLY Accelerate the "Flow of Life" process when our thoughts and feelings are all in HARMONY with ONE ANOTHER, making our energy focus in a single direction (a single phase).

    When energy is scattered, going out it all directions, parts of our energy are in conflict with other thoughts (beliefs) in our subconscious mind. The Scattered Energy directly affects how quickly Directed Energy can complete its mission, and return back to the sender.

3. **"Psycho-Cybernetics"** – an insightful book by Dr. Maxwell Maltz. In it, he shared his discovery that not only does our mind have memory, but also all the cells of our body temple have memory.

    Because this information was clearly verified in the author's "Bubble Experience," all affirmations and all forgiveness processes are stated to be most effective and most efficient when stated OUT LOUD!

Ron Palumbo's Empowerment Workshops

Email: ronpalumbo@outlook.com
Website: rpalumbo.com

To Attend and/or Host "Using the Law of Attraction WISELY" Workshop

To attend our workshop in your city, or in a city near you, or to plant the seeds for Ron bring Empowerment Workshops to your city, contact Ron in any of the following ways:

P O Box 112, Gladwin MI 48624

Email: **ronpalumbo@outlook.com**

Website: **UsingtheLawofAttractionWISELY.com**

Ron has facilitated Law of Attraction Workshops in many different settings, including Corporate offices, Chiropractic Offices, churches, community colleges, community centers, and in many individual homes.

To Host our Law of Attraction workshop or any of our Empowerment Programs in your area, including in the comfortable setting of your home (for family and friends) - contact Ron.

Professional Services Available

Interactive Workshops –insightful, empowering workshops on several topics including: The Law of Attraction (also available on a 3-CD Album), healing, enhancing relationships, success; Bible Metaphysics, etc.

Intensives – usually a multi-day event where one is immersed in the utilization and practice of Spiritual Principle covering various life areas, such as physical healing; effectively S-L-O-W-I-N-G the aging process; focused energy work; deep healing meditations; abundance; enhancing relationships; etc.

Group Healing Sessions – a deep-healing meditation plus individual energy work for each person in our group.

Group Meditation – a time of deep relaxation and total peace. This allows our body temple the "down time" needed to renew, rejuvenate, and regenerate the body's cells.

* Couples Counseling – helps bring clarity to your primary relationship, offering tools to greatly enhance and strengthen all your relationships, especially your primary relationship. It also helps in bringing more love and more nurturing into your primary relationship. *** (This can be a Long Distance service).**

* Transitioning A Relationship – a process that helps couples change their relationship from "Romantic" to a "Friendship" relationship. *** (can be L.D.)**

* Counseling Sessions – for individuals, couples, and/or families seeking clarity on various life areas including: family dynamics; releasing Old Hurts; guidance and/or direction in a particular life area; family co-operation; and more. *** (can be L.D. service)**

* Life Coaching – for support, guidance, and direction in moving through barriers and challenges and to experience higher levels of self-worth, self-love, & self-mastery, all of which results in being MORE EMPOWERED, improved work performance, and living life more abundantly. *** (This can be a Long Distance service).**

* Private Healing Session – includes a time of Deep Relaxation Meditation followed by energy work, both of which help the renewing and healing process allowing cells and organs to revitalized. *** (can be L.D. service).**

* All Long Distance services can be done by phone, so location is never an issue.